The Martyrdom of St Phokas of Sinope

Texts from Christian Late Antiquity

31

Series Editor

George Anton Kiraz

TeCLA (Texts from Christian Late Antiquity) is a series presenting ancient Christian texts both in their original languages and with accompanying contemporary English translations.

The Martyrdom of St Phokas of Sinope

The Syriac Version

Introduction, translation and edition by
Sebastian P. Brock

gorgias press
2013

Gorgias Press LLC, 954 River Road, Piscataway, NJ, 08854, USA

www.gorgiaspress.com

Copyright © 2013 by Gorgias Press LLC

All rights reserved under International and Pan-American Copyright Conventions. No part of this publication may be reproduced, stored in a retrieval system or transmitted in any form or by any means, electronic, mechanical, photocopying, recording, scanning or otherwise without the prior written permission of Gorgias Press LLC.

2013

ISBN 978-1-4632-0189-0   ISSN 1935-6846

Library of Congress Cataloging-in-Publication Data

A Cataloging-in-Publication Record is Available from the Library of Congress.

Printed in the United States of America

TABLE OF CONTENTS

Table of Contents v
Preface ix
Abbreviations xi
Introduction 1
    Sources 2
    Outline of the Martyrdom 4
    The Syriac translation of the Martyrdom 6
    The date of the commemoration of St Phokas 8
    Some major differences between the Syriac (= Armenian)
        and the Greek 11
    Corruptions in A and B 11
    The treatment of biblical references and allusions 13
    Orthography 14
    The Syriac text 15
Translation 17
    The Martyrdom of Phokas who made his witness in
        Sinope on 13th October. 17
Syriac Text 35
Bibliography 55
    Ancient texts 55
    Modern literature 55
Index of Names 57
Index of Biblical References 59
Index of Greek Words 61

Dedicated to

A.A.M. Bryer

ΦΙΛΙΑΣ ΚΑΙ ΤΙΜΗΣ ΕΝΕΚΕΝ

PREFACE

In their monumental two-volume *The Byzantine Monuments and Topography of the Pontos* Anthony Bryer and David Winfield commented at one point that 'the real patron of the mariners and the merchants of the city [sc. of Sinope] was Phokas, the gardener and first bishop of Sinop'.[1] Although the historical identity of this martyr remains elusive, the cult of St Phokas of Sinope (modern Sinop), as a patron saint of mariners, was already widespread by the end of the fourth century. The earliest surviving witnesses to the Acts of his martyrdom happen to be two Syriac manuscripts, one of the fifth/sixth century, the other of the sixth/seventh century; these contain a Syriac translation of a Greek original text, which has otherwise come down to us only in manuscripts of a much later date. In view of the early date of these two witnesses, whose existence has hitherto been ignored in discussions of the sources on St Phokas, it has seemed worthwhile to make their text available in an edited form, accompanied by a translation and brief introduction.

I take the opportunity to dedicate this small contribution on this Pontic saint, *hestiatōr* to seafarers, to the Symposiarch of many a Spring Byzantine Symposium and great connoisseur of all matters to do with the Pontus, Anthony Bryer, Emeritus Professor of Byzantine Studies in the University of Birmingham, whose energy, backed by his 'infectious and all-encompassing enthusiasm' (John Haldon), not only led to the inauguration of the annual Byzantine Symposia in Britain (1966–) and the establishment of a Centre for Byzantine Studies at the University of Birmingham (1975), but has

---

[1] (Washington DC, 1985), I, p.71.

also been the inspiration for a fresh renewal of interest in Byzantine Studies in Great Britain (and elsewhere).[2]

I would also like to thank Melonie Schmierer-Lee of Gorgias Press for her skilful work in bringing this volume to publication.

---

[2] See the tributes in L. Brubaker and K. Linardou (eds), *'Eat, Drink and be Merry' (Luke 12:19). Food and Wine in Byzantium. Papers of the 37th Annual Spring Symposium of Byzantine Studies in Honour of Professor A.A.M. Bryer* (Aldershot, 2007), pp. 3–23.

ABBREVIATIONS

BHG   *Bibliotheca Hagiographica Graeca*, ed. F. Halkin (³1957; Novum Auctarium, 1984).
BHL   *Bibliotheca Hagiographica Latina*, I–II (1898–1901; ²Suppl. 1911).
BHO   *Bibliotheca Hagiographica Orientalis*, ed. P. Peeters (1910).
PG   *Patrologia Graeca.*
PL   *Patrologia Latina.*
PO   *Patrologia Orientalis.*

INTRODUCTION

Towards the end of the fifth century, in the Syrian village of Basufan to the north west of Aleppo, the following inscription was erected to commemorate the building of a shrine dedicated to St Phokas:[3]

> Praise to our Lord! Let there be a good commemoration for the Periodeutes Damianos who set up this shrine to St Phokas. We began on the building in the year 540 and we completed it in 544. The deacon Daniel the st[eward?] of the community. May their commemoration be for a blessing.

The dates, by the era of Antioch, correspond to 491/2 and 495/6. Approximately contemporary with this inscription, a Syriac scribe, working in an unknown location, copied out the Syriac translation of the Martyrdom of St Phokas. Probably less than a century later another Syriac scribe copied out the same text again. These two manuscripts, which are here edited and translated, happen to be the earliest surviving witnesses to the dossier of this once popular saint whose miraculous protection of seafarers was mentioned by (among others)[4] Severus, Patriarch of Antioch, in a homily preached in Antioch in June 515.[5]

---

[3] H. Pognon, *Inscriptions sémitiques* (Paris, 1907), pp. 60–1 (no. 21).
[4] Notably John Chrysostom, on the arrival of his relics in Constantinople, c. 403 (PG 50, cols 699-706), and Gregory of Nazianzus, in one of his poems (PG 37, col. 1486A).
[5] Homily 72, ed. M. Brière, PO 12:1 (1915), p. 87.

Sources

Details concerning the person of Phokas are confused, and three main groups of texts concerning him offer conflicting information:

1. Phokas was a gardener whose cultivated land lay just outside the city gate of Sinope, on the Black Sea coast of Turkey. He had a reputation for hospitality, and when he was denounced as a Christian during the persecutions, he entertained those who had been sent to arrest him; when they asked where they would find Phokas, he pointed to himself, and thus was martyred. He was subsequently seen as a protector of sailors in distress at sea. This information was already known to, and given by, Asterius, bishop of Amasea (the metropolitan see of Sinope), in a sermon which is likely to date from about 400.[6] There is no mention of Phokas being a bishop, and no indication of any date. Phokas the gardener features in the Synaxarium Constantinopolitanum in the first of two notices on 22nd September.[7]

2. Phokas was the first bishop of Sinope who was martyred under Trajan. In passing it is mentioned that he had been a ship's pilot. The detailed account of his trial before the governor Africanus, and then before Trajan himself, ending with his martyrdom, indirectly purports to be by an eyewitness.[8] This Martyrdom is known in Greek,[9] which is the

---

[6] *BHG* 1538; Homily 4, ed. C. Datema, *Asterius of Amasea, Homilies I-XIV* (Leiden, 1970), pp. 114–27; English translation by B. Dehandschutter in J. Leemans and others (eds), *Greek Homilies on Christian Martyrs* (London, 2003), pp. 167–73.

[7] Ed. H. Delehaye, *Synaxarium Ecclesiae Constantinopolitanae e codice Sirmondiano* (Bruxelles, 1902), cols 67–9.

[8] Thus in section 46 'fear fell on *us*', and in 74 the Syriac and Armenian have '*we* entered the prison' (the Greek has 'they').

[9] *BHG* 1536. The text is edited in the *Acta Sanctorum, Mensis Iulius III* (Antwerp, 1723), pp. 639–45.

INTRODUCTION 3

source of the present Syriac translation; Armenian,[10] Georgian,[11] and Latin[12] translations also survive. In the Synaxarium Constantinopolitanum this Phokas is commemorated on 22nd July (the name of his see, however, is not mentioned).[13]

3. Phokas was the son of the ship-builder Pamphilus and Maria (or Makaria) in Heraklea, who went on to perform miracles in saving people at sea; he was eventually ordained deacon, priest and then bishop. His martyrdom was announced by a dove which alighted on him, placing a crown on his head. No details are given of his martyrdom, and there is no indication of any date when it occurred. This 'Life' is known in slightly different forms in both Greek[14] and Armenian[15]. He features in the Synaxarium Constantinopolitanum in the second of the two notices on 22nd

---

[10] *BHO* 990; edited in *Vark' ew vkayabanutiwnk' srboc,'* II (Venice, 1874), pp. 491–502. English translation by F.C. Conybeare, in his *The Armenian Apology and Acts of Apollonius and other Monuments of Early Christianity* (2nd edn, London, 1896), pp. 87–121.

[11] See M. Tarchnišvili, *Geschichte der kirchlichen georgischen Literatur* (Testi e Studi 185; 1955), p.490 (cf. 97); also G, Garitte, *Le calendrier palestino-géorgien du Sinaiticus 34 (Xe siècle)* (Subsidia Hagiographica 30; Bruxelles, 1958), pp.263, 299, 337. One of the earliest depictions of St Phokas is to be found in the eleventh-century church of the Dormition in Lychne, in western Georgia (modern Abkhazia); the well-preserved depiction of him as a bishop (identified by an inscription in Georgian) is illustrated in E. Constantinides, *Images from the Byzantine Periphery* (Leiden, 2007), Plates, 9.32.

[12] *BHL* 6838 (II, p. 994); commemorated in several western calendars on 14th July.

[13] Ed. Delehaye, cols 835–6.

[14] *BHG* 1535y and 1535z; these were edited by C. van de Vorst, 'Saint Phocas', *Analecta Bollandiana* 30 (1911), pp. 272–9, and 279–84 respectively.

[15] *BHO* 991, edited in *Vark' ew vkayabanutiwnk' srboc',* II (Venice, 1874), pp. 485–90. Latin translation by P. Peeters *apud* van de Vorst, 'Saint Phocas', pp. 291–5.

September.[16]

What at first sight looks like a fourth Phokas, described as a martyr of Antioch, is mentioned in the Martyrologium Hieronymianum (with many western derivatives, including the calendar of Bede). This is very probably based on a misunderstanding arising from the presence of some of Phokas of Sinope's relics in Antioch.[17]

Following the study of the dossier of Phokas by Van de Vorst,[18] it has generally been accepted[19] that all these different texts concern one and the same person, each representing a different stage in the process of remedying the lack of any real historical information about this saint whose cult had already become widespread by the beginning of the fifth century.

OUTLINE OF THE MARTYRDOM

The Martyrdom falls into several disparate parts:

1–3   Introduction. The author states that he is writing to 'brethren in Pontus, Bithynia, Paphagonia, Mysia, Galatia, Cappadocia and Armenia'[20] to inform them of the ex-

---

[16] Ed. Delehaye, cols 69–70. Here he has been associated with Sinope, and his martyrdom is said to have been by the sword (so Phokas 1, above) and fire (so Phokas 2, above), and under Trajan (so Phokas 2).

[17] According to Gregory of Tours, *The Glory of the Martyrs*, 98 (PL 71, col 791; English translation, R. Van Dam, Liverpool, 1988), he 'rests in Syria' (*apud Syriam requiescit*). This Phokas is commemorated in several western calendars on 5th March.

[18] C. van de Vorst, 'Saint Phocas', *Analecta Bollandiana* 30 (1911), pp.252-95; some further information was provided by A. Erhard in his notice in *Byzantinische Zeitschrift* 21 (1912/3), pp. 309–11. As van de Vorst pointed out, the fourteenth-century Pontic author Andreas Libadenos treated the gardener and the bishop as a single person.

[19] Notably by W. Enslin, in Pauly-Wissowa, *Realenzyklopädie* 20 (1940), p. 451–2; N.A. Oikonomides, Ὁ Ἅγιος Φωκᾶς ὁ Σινωπεύς, *Archeion Pontou* 17 (1952), pp. 184–219, and J-M. Sauget, in *Bibliotheca Sanctorum* V (Rome, 1964), cols 948–50.

[20] Thus in both the Syriac and Armenian; the place names are absent from the Greek.

ploits of the martyr Phokas, whose way of life - and that of other martyrs – should serve as a model.

4–48 Phokas is brought before the Governor, Africanus, who attempts to get him to sacrifice to the pagan gods. Apart from brief narrative sections at the beginning and end (4; 46–8), this part is entirely given over to the altercation between Phokas and Africanus. In the course of the dialogue it emerges that Phokas is a bishop (13). At the end of this section an earthquake occurs, accompanied by other phenomena, and Africanus falls down, seemingly dead. His distraught wife, Terentina, then appears, and begs Phokas to restore him. Having summoned his clergy Phokas prays over him and he revives, whereupon he sends message of his deliverance to the emperor.

49–68 Phokas is now interrogated by the emperor Trajan. The altercation is briefly interrupted in 59, after Phokas has asked to see Trajan's gods; the two men go into a temple, and Phokas addresses one of the gods directly, asking the statue if it wants something to eat or drink (60). The dialogue with Trajan then continues (61–68) and in passing Phokas mentions that he had been a sailor.

69–74 Narrative resumes. Phokas is tortured and he prays in silence, after which a voice from heaven is heard, encouraging him and threatening Trajan. Trajan orders his imprisonment. Phokas' midnight prayer is given (72–3) at the end of which the prison doors fall open and the astonished guards ask for baptism; this duly takes place on the sea shore.

75–90 The next morning Phokas is again summoned before Trajan, and large crowds gather in expectation. A further altercation between Phokas and Trajan takes place (76–83), ending with Trajan ordering that he be thrown into a lime pit, and then, when Phokas emerged unharmed, he has him thrown into the specially heated baths. After a final short prayer, Phokas finally dies. When the baths were opened his remains were found 'like beautiful nard', at which Trajan exclaims that 'there is no other God'. Phokas then appears to him threateningly, as a result of

	which Trajan, back in his palace, collapses and expires, being 'eaten by worms'.
91	A final paragraph tells of his renown among sea-farers, and the extent of his fame.

Although Conybeare made a valiant attempt to argue for the historicity of the Martyrdom, his arguments have not stood up to criticism from van de Vorst and others. The fictitious character of the Martyrdom is clear, and numerous parallels to motifs could be found in other legendary martyrdoms. The New Testament will also have suggested a number of features: thus, for example, Pilate's wife is likely to have been the model for Terentina, the release of Paul and Silas from prison for Phokas' miraculous release, and Herod's fate for the death of Trajan. What is unusual is the ironic introduction of the names of Aristotle and Demosthenes.

THE SYRIAC TRANSLATION OF THE MARTYRDOM

In the various discussions of the dossier, the existence of two very early witnesses to a Syriac translation of the Greek Martyrdom (designated as the 'Passio' in BHG) has apparently been overlooked.[21] These two witnesses are both to be found in Vatican Syriac 160, a composite manuscript that incorporates three originally separate manuscripts, all from between the fifth and the seventh century:

ff.1–79: I.	The Life of Symeon the Stylite. This section of the manuscript is dated 17th Nisan 521 of the era of Antioch, corresponding to 17th April AD 474. The text was already edited in the eighteenth century by S. E. Assemani, in his *Acta Sanctorum et Martyrum*.[22]

---

[21] The same applies to the Georgian version, transmitted in a number of manuscripts: see above, note 11.

[22] II, (Rome, 1748), pp. 268–394. There is a recent English translation by R. Doran, *The Lives of Simeon Stylites* (Kalamazoo, 1992), pp. 103–98.

ff.80–219:II. Select lives of saints, including Phokas (ff. 205r–211r,[23] = A). In S. E. and J. S. Assemani's *Catalogus* the manuscript is dated to the 10th century,[24] but this is far too late: the small neat estrangelo hand is very similar to that of the earliest dated Syriac manuscript, British Library Add. 12,150, written in Edessa and dated November (AD) 411.[25] As several more recent scholars have observed, it would thus seem preferable to date this section of the manuscript to the fifth, or at latest, sixth century.[26]

ff.220–239: III. Select lives of saints, including Phokas (ff.224v–231v, = B). The estrangelo hand is rather larger and is typical of a number of hands firmly dated to the sixth century; in any case it can hardly be later than the seventh century.

As will be discussed in more detail below, these two witnesses, A and B, to the Martyrdom both represent the same translation of a Greek text that was closely related to, but by no means identical with, that printed in the *Acta Sanctorum*. B was definitely not copied from A for it sometimes preserves better readings; furthermore it has also often preserved an older orthography. In a few places where the Syriac has a longer or shorter text than the Greek, or a

---

[23] The foliation of ff. 206–8 is in disorder, with ff. 206 and 208 interchanged.

[24] *Bibliothecae Apostolicae Vaticanae codicum manuscriptorum Catalogus* III (Rome, 1759; repr. Paris, 1926), pp. 319–28, here, 328.

[25] W.H.P. Hatch, *An Album of Dated Syriac Manuscripts* (Boston, 1945; repr. with additional preface by L. van Rompay, Piscataway NJ, forthcoming), plate I.

[26] E. Tisserant was even inclined to date it to the first quarter of the fifth century, thus very close to the date of Asterius: see his magisterial article 'Nestorienne, (L'Église), in *Dictionnaire de Théologie Catholique* 11 (1931), cols 157–323, here col. 166. For a brief discussion, opting for 5th/6th-century dating, see G. Wiessner, *Zur Märtyrerüberlieferung aus der Christenverfolgung Schapurs II* (Abhandlungen der Akademie der Wissenschaften in Göttingen, phil.-hist. Klasse, III.67; 1967), p. 9, note 2.

different one, it finds support in the Armenian translation; although this at first sight might suggest that the Armenian was translated from the Syriac, rather than directly from Greek, this is definitely not the case;[27] thus the Syriac and Armenian can be seen as two independent witnesses to the Greek text.

THE DATE OF THE COMMEMORATION OF ST PHOKAS

A striking difference in the dating of the commemoration of the saint is to be found in the heading of the Syriac text, where both manuscripts give the date of his martyrdom as the 13th October. This does not correspond with either of the two Greek dates (22nd September, 22nd July),[28] though it is to be found in a pair of Syrian Orthodox calendars,[29] and probably in the Chronicle *ad annum* 846, where, however, the month, Teshri I (October), has been corrupted to Teshri II (November); this Chronicle provides the following notice among the events of Trajan's reign:[30]

> During these times the holy Mar Phokas, bishop and martyr, was martyred; he was of the same rank as the Apostles. He was martyred on 13th Teshri II in 'SPWNY' (a corruption of Sinope (SYNWP').

Despite the difference of month (November, instead of October), this cannot properly be treated as an independent witness, since the description of Phokas as 'of the same rank as the Apostles' is clearly derived from the final paragraph of the Syriac Martyrdom.

---

[27] Numerous examples can be found where the Armenian translation must be based on a Greek text, and not the Syriac translation.

[28] Not surprisingly, the Greek dates are to be found in Melkite Synaxaria: see J-M. Sauget, *Premières recherches sur l'origine et les caractéristiques des synaxaires melkites (XIe-XVII siècles* (Subsidia Hagiographica 45; Bruxelles, 1969). pp. 119, 155.

[29] Paris Syr. 146 and Vatican Syr. 69, in F. Nau (ed.), *Martyrologes et ménologes orientaux, I-XIII* (PO 10:1, 1912), p. 64. These two calendars also provide the dates of 8th June (p.79) and 22 July (p.82) for 'the martyr Phokas'; this last date is also found in British Library Add. 17,232 (p. 123).

[30] E.W. Brooks (ed.), *Chronica Minora* II (CSCO Scr. Syri 3, repr. 1960), p. 183.

In the fourteenth-century calendar of Rabban Saliba, 'Phokas (patron) for those who travel by sea', is commemorated on yet a different date, June 1,[31] while two further martyrs with the name Phokas feature there on 21st and 22nd September; the latter was martyred with 'his disciples' while with the former it is stated that 'a dove spoke with him in a human voice', possibly a reference to the dove which announced his martyrdom in the 'Life'. While the Phokas of June 1 is certainly to be identified as the Phokas of Sinope, the other may well reflect the influence of the Greek date of 22nd September.

An added complication lies in the relationship of St Phokas with the Maronite St Nuhra: according to the calendars of Vatican Syr. 313 and of al-Qila'i, they are commemorated on the same day, 22nd July. For this date the calendar in Paris Syr 146 has just Phokas, but the closely related calendar of Vatican Syr. 46 has instead 'Nuhra', which led Sauget to state that in Vatican Syr. 313 the appearance of St Nuhra ('Light') alongside St Phokas was simply a 'dédoublement',[32] based on a popular etymology of Phokas' name, linking it with *phōs*, 'light' - a link which interestingly is also to be found in BHG 1535, where, at his birth, Phokas' mother exclaims 'a true light (*phōs*) has appeared for us, our firstborn son'.[33] St Nuhra is a very popular saint in Lebanon, especially in the region of Batrun, where he is said to have preached and been martyred;[34] any further information, however, about him seems to be lacking, and his origin and relationship to St Phokas remains mysterious.

---

[31] This is supported by two other calendars in Nau's collection: Add. 17,234, Nau, p. 33; and Add. 14,504, Nau, p. 41.

[32] J-M. Sauget, 'Le calendrier maronite du manuscrit Vatican syriaque 313', *Orientalia Christiana Periodica* 33 (1967), p. 282, note 32.

[33] Ed. van de Vorst, *Analecta Bollandiana* 30 (1911), p.272. Modern scholars, more philologically-minded, have preferred to link the saint's name with *phōkes*, 'seals': see Oikonomides, 'Hagios Phōkas', pp. 194–201.

[34] He is said to have come from Manhur in Persia. The various popular cults are mentioned by J-M. Fiey, 'De quelques saints vénérés au Liban', *Proche Orient Chrétien* 28 (1978), pp. 23–4; see also his *Saints syriaques* (ed. L.I. Conrad; Princeton, 2004), p.146. G. Graf mentions the existence of a Garshuni Life of St Nuhra in his *Geschichte der christlichen arabischen Literatur*, I (Studi et Testi 118; 1944), p. 529.

Given the many different dates in the various calendars, eastern and western, on which a commemoration of St Phokas is to be found, it will be helpful to list them in the sequence of the Syriac liturgical calendar where the year begins with October:

Oct. 13:	Syriac Martyrdom; Paris syr 146 & Vatican syr. 69; Maronite Calendar of Ibn al-Qila'i.
Oct 15:	Maronite Calendar in Vat. Syr. 313.
Nov. 13:	Syriac Chronicle to 846 [Teshri II in error for Teshri I]
Jan. 5 (10 Tubeh):	'Synaxaire arabe jacobite':[35] 'bishop of Pontus under Hadrian(!)', but details of his martrydom are from the Martyrdom, BHG 1536.
Mar. 5:	Martyrologium Hieronymanum and Romanum (and western derivatives): 'Phocas of Antioch'.
Jun. 1:	Calendar of R. Saliba; Br. Libr., Add. 14504, 17134.
Jun. 8:	Paris Syr. 146, Vatican Syr. 69.
Jul. 11:	Melkite calendar according to al-Biruni.[36]
Jul. 14:	Martyrologium Hieronymanum and Romanum (and western derivatives):[37] 'Phocas bishop of Pontus, martyred under Trajan'.
Jul. 22:	Synaxarium Constantinopolitanum; Syrian Orthodox calendars in Paris Syr. 146, Vat. Syr. 69, and Br. Libr., Add. 17,232; Maronite calendars of Vat. Syr. 313 and al-Qila'i (also the modern Maronite calendar).

---

[35] Ed. R. Basset, PO 11:5 (1916), pp. 537–9.
[36] Ed. R. Griveau, PO 10:3, p. 23.
[37] Including the Old English Martyrology (ed. G. Kotzor), where he is described as 'bishop of Pontus', martyred under Trajan; some more details, derived from the Martyrium, are given in the Calendar of Bede, which also states that his relics are preserved in Vienne (France): cf. *Analecta Bollandiana* 49 (1931), p. 75.

Jul. 23   Greek Synaxarion in Christ Church ms (transfer of
(17 Hrotits): his relics);[38] Armenian Synaxarion[39] (with details
             derived from the Martyrium).

Sep. 21:   Calendar of Rabban Saliba.

Sep. 22:   Synaxarium Constantinopolitanum; Calendar of
             Rabban Saliba.

SOME MAJOR DIFFERENCES BETWEEN THE SYRIAC (= ARMENIAN) AND THE GREEK

On a number of occasions the Syriac and Armenian translations have material that is not present in the Greek; this applies, for example, to the extra geographical names, indicating the popularity of the cult of Phokas, in sections 1 and 91. Extra material in the two versions is to be found in the second half of sections 2 and 35, while the entire sections 22–3 and 40–41 are absent from the Greek. In section 72, in particular, there are many differences, with the Greek providing a longer text earlier in the section, but lacking material in the Syriac and Armenian towards the end of it. At the beginning of 76 the Syriac has lost some text, no doubt through homoioteleuton; whether this goes back to the translator or to a common ancestor of A and B is impossible to tell. Sections 83 and 84 of the Syriac are present in the Greek, but are missing from the Armenian. It should be noticed that there are also several other places where the Syriac agrees with the Greek, against the Armenian (e.g. at the beginning of section 4).

CORRUPTIONS IN A AND B

Many of the seemingly more significant differences between A and B are due to corruptions in one or other manuscript; in most cases either the context or the Greek original (or both) will indicate

---

[38] See also F. Halkin, 'Le synaxaire grec de Christ Church à Oxford', *Analecta Bollandiana* 66 (1948), pp. 85–6; the 23rd is also found in Nikodemos of the Holy Mountain, Συναξαρίστης, III (Venice, 1819; repr. Athens, 2005), p. 361.

[39] Ed. G. Bayan, PO 21:6 (1930), pp. 765–6.

which of the two manuscripts has preserved the correct text. As will be seen from the following selection of more striking examples, neither manuscript is free from such corruptions:

(a)   corruption in A] B = Greek

      3
      16
      49
      71
      72
      74

In the edition of the text, all such readings in B have been adopted in the text.

(b)   A = Greek] corruption in B

      1
      1
      46
      72
      72
      72
      89

Many of these corruptions are due to transpositions or straightforward misreadings, and there are no traces of any evidence for a revision of the original translation based on subsequent consultation of the Greek text.

One variant in B is intriguing: at 55 A has 'Were you summoned to sacrifice or to do philosophy?' (*d-pilsoputa te'bed*); B has made a slight alteration, *d-pilsopise te'bed*, 'to philosophize', introducing a hellenizing construction consisting of a Greek aorist infinitive (here *philosophēsai*) followed by *'bad* (or, with aorist passive infinitive, *hwa*). This construction, found with a number of verbs, including this one, became not uncommon in certain texts in the sixth century; its presence in a hagiographical text is, however, surprising, and its introduction here by the scribe of B suggests that he was also familiar with copying more learned texts as well.

THE TREATMENT OF BIBLICAL REFERENCES AND ALLUSIONS

Usually in earlier Syriac translations from Greek the biblical quotations are adapted to that of the Syriac Bible (normally, Peshitta). Though most of the explicit quotations are too short and lacking in any diagnostic differences between the Greek and Peshitta, there does seem to be a deliberate use of the Peshitta's wording for I Cor. 1:19, below.

17 Dan. 2:21 ܗܘ ܕܝܗܒ ܚܟܡܬܐ ܠܚܟܝ̈ܡܐ

This translates the Greek word for word, and happens to conform exactly with the Peshitta.

I Cor. 3:19 ܐܝܟ ܕܐܡܝܪ ܠܚܟܝ̈ܡܐ ܒܢ̈ܟܠܬܗܘܢ

The Peshitta ends the phrase with ܒܚܪܥܘܬܗܘܢ

I Cor. 1:19 ܐܘܒܕ ܚܟܡܬܐ ܕܚܟܝ̈ܡܐ ܘܐܣܠܐ
ܬܪܥܝܬܐ ܕܣܘܟܠܬܢ̈ܐ

This corresponds exactly with the Peshitta, where the word order is different from the Greek of both the quotation and the Greek New Testament.

27 I Cor. 1:23–4 ܠܝܗܘܕ̈ܝܐ ܬܘܩܠܬܐ ܘܠܥܡ̈ܡܐ ܣܟܠܘܬܐ.
ܠܢ ܕܝܢ ܡܗܝ̈ܡܢܐ ܡܫܝܚܐ ܚܝܠܐ ܗܘ
ܕܐܠܗܐ ܘܚܟܡܬܐ

Though slightly abbreviated and adapted (e.g. 'to us'), this corresponds closely both to the Greek of the Martyrdom and to the Peshitta, where only difference lies in the choice of ܣܟܠܘܬܐ instead of ܫܛܝܘܬܐ ; this will be due to the occurrence of ܣܟܠܘܬܐ in the previous section, and the agreement with the reading of the Harklean here will be purely fortuitous.

35 I Sam. 2:6 ܐܢܐ ܡܡܝܬ ܐܢܐ ܘܐܢܐ ܡܚܐ ܐܢܐ

Although the words are attributed to Christ, the source of the quotation seems likely to be I Sam. 2:6 (the Song of Hannah), where the statement appears in the third person with God as subject. The awkwardness of the mention of 'Christ' (clearly likely to be the original reading) has been noticed in both the Greek and the Armenian, which replace 'Christ' by 'God', and for good measure the Greek further adds 'through the prophet'.

64   Mt. 7:6   ܠܐ ܬܪܡܘܢ (ܕܘ̈ܪܬܟܘܢ) ܩܕܡ ܚܙܝܪ̈ܐ ܡܪ̈ܓܢܝܬܟܘܢ

The reading of A, ܬܪܡܘܢ, corresponds exactly with the Peshitta (and Old Syriac). Although at first sight this might suggest that A's reading goes back to the translator, such an explanation would leave B's reading without a satisfactory explanation; thus it seems more likely that B's reading represents the original text of the Syriac translation here, while A's reading is secondary, having been adapted at a secondary stage to the Peshitta's text.

Of the various biblical allusions, one deserves particular comment. In 7, where the Greek text simply has 'God in heaven', the Syriac translator has substituted 'the dweller in heaven', a phrase he will have derived from the Peshitta of I and II Maccabees where it occurs several times (see annotation *ad locum*), being based on Psalm 123(122):1.

ORTHOGRAPHY

In a number of places B alone provides the plene forms, ܡܛܘܠ and ܗܘܐ,[40] instead of the standard ܡܛܠ and ܗܘ; these fuller forms, characteristic of a number of early manuscripts, become very rare in manuscripts after about the sixth century.[41] A further archaic spelling found only in B is ܐܠܗܘܐ in place of ܐܠܗܐ (90, 3).

In a number of other cases, older forms occur inconsistently, now in A, now in B. Thus A provides the prosthetic *alaph* (rare later) in ܐܪܙܘܢܐ (1), while for the passive forms of weak verbs the older spelling is found first in A, and then later in B:

53   ܡܬܚܙܒ = A (B ܡܬܚܝܙܒ)

80   ܬܬܝܗܒ = B (A ܬܬܗܒ).

---

[40] The former features in 13 (twice), 31, 39 and 82; the latter in 1, 3 (twice), 5, 12, 43 and 45.

[41] See my 'Some diachronic features of Classical Syriac', in M.F.J. Baasten and W.Th. van Peursen (eds), *Hamlet on a Hill: Semitic and Greek Studies presented to Professor T. Muraoka* (Orientalia Lovaniensia Orientalia 118; 2003), pp. 95–111, esp. 96–7.

A similar inconsistency is found with the old form ܐܢܫܝܢ, instead of ܐܢܫ:

63   ܐܢܫܝܢ = A (B ܐܢܫ)

although:

65   ܐܢܫܝܢ = B (A ܐܢܫ)

B furthermore adds the old form in 1 and 60.

Nor is there any consistency in either manuscript over the use of shortened participial forms; thus we find:

6   ܩܕܡ ܐܝܬ = A; ܡܩܕܡ B

although:

13   ܒܝܬ = A; ܐܝܬ ܒܗ B.

Greek names have sometimes been better preserved in B; this is especially the case with Demosthenes, whose name has been seriously debased in A at 38. B has a tendency to provide forms of Greek names and loanwords in shorter forms: thus, whereas A normally has ܐܦܪܝܩܢܘܣ for Africanus, B prefers ܐܦܪܩܢܘܣ; and for the loanword *politeia* B provides ܦܘܠܝܛܐ, against A's ܦܘܠܝܛܝܐ.

An archaic feature is the frequent absence of a point above participial forms (this feature has been kept in the edition).

The Syriac text

For the edition of the Syriac text, the text of A has been used as the basis, on the grounds that it is the older manuscript; variant readings (other than orthographic) in B are given in the apparatus. Where, however, a comparison with the Greek original indicates that it is B which has preserved the better text, then the readings of B have been adopted into the text, and such places are clearly distinguished in the apparatus, where the information takes the form: '= B; A ....'. In a few places both manuscripts are evidently corrupt and the text has been corrected; in such cases the apparatus is in the form: 'cj [conjecture]; A B ...'.

Section numbers have been added for convenience of reference. For the most part these correspond to the major punctuation marks in A (three small circles, the centre black and the two outer ones red). Since the minor punctuation is rather sparse in the manuscripts, here and there, for ease of reading, I have added some further punctuation.

Apart from the orthographical differences noted above, small variants of a purely orthographical nature have not been included in the apparatus.

The English translation is deliberately on the literal side, so as to facilitate comparison with the Greek and the Armenian.

TRANSLATION

In the translation which follows, new paragraph numbers have been supplied for convenience; roman numerals in square brackets represent the earlier numbers of the edition of the Greek text in the *Acta Sanctorum* (also used by Conybeare in his translation of the Armenian).

THE MARTYRDOM OF PHOKAS WHO MADE HIS WITNESS IN SINOPE ON 13TH OCTOBER.

1. [I] Concerning those who (were) after the divine epiphany of that Epiphany of ours, our Lord Jesus Christ, and at the coming of Him who did not tire, (who) is merciful, mighty, a Physician, Shepherd, and Teacher, God, Lord of renowned conduct: upright, ineffable, unattainable, and without spot is the mystery of those who hold their hope rightly,[1] and are sealed with the seal of the Christians, and amidst many diverse afflictions, with fasting and persecution, in flight and in constancy, in insult and in glory, in suffering and in life, many times over they have rightly and without rebuke been named 'like angels', 'apostles'; and they have suffered by means of the renowned and glorious contest of martyrdom - people who[2] have handed down to us a type of all that our Lord Jesus Christ suffered, (doing so) through their faith[3] which is without reproach, they

---

[1] A = Greek; B 'those whose hope is upright'. The syntax of this paragraph in Syriac is often obscure.

[2] B 'which they'.

[3] A = Greek, Armenian; B 'our faith'.

being steadfast. And thus they have proclaimed to us, to everyone and to every location, an adorned and glorious conduct (*politeia*): people who, in athletic renown, were fulfilled (as) martyrs with judicial sentences, them will I make known to you in this my book, O brethren who dwell in Pontus, Bithynia, Paphlagonia, Mysia, Galatia, Cappadocia, and Armenia,[4] so that you may become imitators of their valour and their struggle. And may we too imitate them [II] as we recall and remember those who <perished> by fire, sword, on the cross, with lacerations of all sorts, in fighting with wild animals, in drowning, in lime (pits), with various kinds of amputations and in torments. And may we be admonished and learn. Great and excellent are the benefits[5] of the Good (God), and we will become partisans in the hope that is through our Lord Jesus Christ, to whom be glory and victory for eternal ages, amen.

2. (This) is especially (well-)known and made manifest to everyone through the valour and perseverance of the martyr Phokas. Not only through the fire and shameful stripes, but also through a chaste and pure and blameless life, a purity and mode of life (*politeia*) that would be his, which took place before the eyes of our Saviour, our Lord Jesus Christ.

Had it been possible for the entire history of his perseverance to be written down with the records and (judicial) sentences, it would not in this way alone have stirred and disturbed those who hear it.[6]

3. The manner of life of the blessed Phokas is as follows: When he was a child he was <not> caused to stumble by the destructive Serpent; rather, he was pure and blameless like one of our Lord's doves.[7] From his youth onward he took His yoke upon his shoulders[8] with awe. As a man, he

---

[4] 'who dwell in Pontus...Armenia': = Armenian; om. Greek
[5] B 'recollections'.
[6] = Armenian; this paragraph is absent from the Greek.
[7] Cf. Mt. 10:16.
[8] Cf. Mt. 11:29.

became well-known to all in the world, for the needy being richly[9] a helper, while correcting and admonishing all who were pure and chaste. He was 'everything for everyone'.[10] The circumstances of his trials and contests no human being can describe as they really were. We, however, have informed you in brief.

4. [III] When many from the flock of Christians were being seized, the destructive Africanus was going around with his friends and relations searching for him as if for a precious stone. In this way he was making investigations about the true believers and the holy Pastor.

5. When (Phokas) came before the tribunal, Africanus the Governor said, 'This is the Phokas who says that the gods do not exist; and he does not acknowledge that the almighty Trajan is a god. Tell me, have not all the enemies perished at (Trajan's) hands? Who else is a god?'

6. Phokas, however, stood there silent. Africanus said to him, 'Aren't you going to say anything in answer to my question to you? Don't you realize where you are standing?'

7. Phokas said to him, 'If you were speaking about the God, the dweller in heaven,[11] you would be acceptable;[12] but if you spoke about a human being, do not imagine in your mind that you will hear any reply from me.'

8. Africanus said, 'Are the rulers of the world not gods?'

9. Phokas said to him, 'Is it not sufficient for Trajan just to be called "emperor"? But you are wanting to call him by a name that is supreme and most excellent of all.'

---

[9] Thus B; the translator evidently misread *plousiois* as *plousiōs*; A has 'readily', thanks to an easy alteration (*'tyr'yt* > *'tyd'yt*).

[10] Cf. I Cor. 10:33.

[11] Greek: 'there is a God in heaven'; the Syriac translator's 'dweller in heaven' reflects the wording found several times in the Syriac translation of I and II Maccabees (e.g. I Macc. 3:18, 50, 60; 4:10 etc; II Macc. 3:30, 7:11 etc.

[12] B 'I would accept it'.

10. [IV] Africanus said to him, 'The Christians are hanging on you as though on a god!'

11. Phokas said to him, 'Far be it that this should enter anyone's mind! In the case of human beings who are fashioned with blood and involved in sins, who are subject to death and are guilty in (their) speech, how(ever) they live, and in whatever way of life, and with whatever deeds, being here (on earth), what action do they have, and in what manner, do they call to mind the invisible God? How is it possible that they should acquire this particular appellation?'

12. Africanus said, 'How, then, did this report concerning you reach the ears of the almighty (emperor)?'

13. Phokas said, 'It is not as if (the report) was about a god, but about a man of God. And as far as this is concerned, it is not because I am[13] anywhere near the excellence of the Apostles of God; for you have also seen me, who am not worthy to be a bishop: it is not as you have said, that I am a god, but people honour me as a pastor of rational sheep. Or is it, maybe, that because you have been entrusted with being a governor by the Lord, for this reason you are wanting to be called a god?'

14. Africanus said, 'A great many advocates are needed to be able to dispute with you!'

15. Phokas said, 'If you bring along advocates from the entire populace, they will not be found to be a match for a single one of God's servants and his disciples.'

16. [V] Africanus said, 'Who would look upon a crucified man as a teacher?'[14]

17. Phokas said to him, 'Consider this majesty and wisdom

---

[13] Both mss have 'because I am not' (*dl'*), which can hardly be right; the translation assumes that *dl'* is a corruption of *d'n'*.

[14] B rightly has 'as a teacher' (*dbrb'*); A has a corruption (*dbbrq'*) 'as in lightning'.

beyond comprehension: if it did not exceed every wisdom that exists, and if all sages had not partaken of it, it would not have been possible for there to have been written "He who gives wisdom to the wise",[15] and again, "He who controls the wise and their devices";[16] and again, "I will destroy the clever ways of the wise, and I will foil the intention of the sages".[17] Do you understand what I am saying?'

18. Africanus said, 'You weren't sent for in order to be asked[18] questions about the law'. And he said, 'But if you do not obey,[19] then you will have come (here) following the imperial law.'

19. Phokas said, 'I am talking to you about the law of God who is invisible, and I am not[20] persuading you, but you are talking with me about a human being who is not[21] similar (to God): today he is, but tomorrow he will die - and would it be that he dies well, and not[22] badly! Do you imagine that you are wanting to persuade me by these things?'

20. Africanus said, 'These words of yours are crafty and devious; cast them on one side, and act wisely about your real life, lest you force me to persuade you by means of many tortures and afflictions.'

21. [VI] Phokas said, 'I am invited to a delightful banquet, so shall I not go to it, especially as its time is close at hand?'

22. Africanus said, 'It is because of this very thing that I am distressed for you.'

---

[15] Dan. 2:21.
[16] I Cor. 3:19 (quoting Job 5:13).
[17] I Cor. 1:19, cf. Is. 29:14.
[18] B 'to ask'.
[19] = B; A 'but if you do'.
[20] B om. 'not'.
[21] B om. 'not'. The Syriac translator has evidently taken *anomou* as *anomoiou*.
[22] Both mss have *l'* 'but'; the translation assumes that this is a corruption of *wl'* (= Greek).

23. Phokas said to him, 'If you were really to have pity on me, you would immediately have done what I want: for you should know that, unless I die, I shall not be able to live (sc. in heaven).'[23]

24. Africanus said, 'Murderers and sorcerers are not worthy to live, but they wish to live, whereas you, with all this 'wisdom' of yours, rely on folly, and you wish to die! I swear by this sun, perhaps you are superior to Aristotle with (all) his philosophy!'

25. Phokas said, 'I have no wish to be a philosopher: my desire is to be a Christian for Christ, for I know that He alone is Lord, and God, and Sovereign. For the philosopher Aristotle taught vain and erroneous things, whereas Christ, the Word of God, has given a way of life of chastity, perseverance and an excellent religion, along with immortality, to those who believe in the one wise God.'[24]

26. Africanus said, 'You have clearly manifested your folly and stupidity by gazing on that crucified man.'

27. Phokas said, 'It is well known that this is a stumbling block for you, for it is written in the law, "For the Jews a stumbling block, but for the Gentiles a folly"[25] - whereas for us believers Christ is the Power of God and Wisdom.'

28. [VII] Africanus said, 'Is there (really) a crucified god?'

29. Phokas said, 'Are there gods and goddesses of stone, and ones that are fabricated? Wicked and carnal people cannot investigate the ways of Jesus Christ.'

30. Africanus said, 'Recollect yourself, and gaze on the zodiac and the varied stars - which you are wanting to leave be-

---

[23] Paragraphs 22 and 23 are absent from the Greek (but present in the Armenian).

[24] = B Greek. A 'and wisdom', in place of B's 'and wise' (i.e. wisdom is also given).

[25] I Cor. 1:23.

hind and die!'

31. Phokas said, 'You have gazed upon the zodiac arrayed with brightness, and on the moon and on the (well-)ordered stars, but you do not enquire into their Maker, and He has not entered your mind, nor do you imagine that He exists. For neither the sun nor the moon is able to make another star; rather, all these things that are visible have come into being at the word of God and of Christ.'

32. Africanus said, 'Are you saying that this light-giver and the heavens came into being from another (being)? And are you refusing them a role?'

33. Phokas said, 'Let this never (be said) that the elements should be called gods!'

34. Africanus said, 'Show me your God, and I will urge the almighty emperor concerning you.'

35. Phokas said, 'Did I not already tell you how God is invisible: He is seated above the heavens, (so) how is it possible for Him to be seen by human beings? But if you want to know God, accompany me, and look how (in the case of) the heaven, the sun,[26] the moon, stars and clouds, it is not heaven which sends down rain when it wants, but when it has been bidden (to do so). And the sun does not give warmth when it wants, but when has been bidden. The moon and the stars give light, not because they want to, but when they are bidden. The clouds do not gather and form at their own wish, but they are brought along as if in orderly formation. Summer does not come when it wants, but when it has been bidden. The sea does not become calm when it wants, nor does it become disturbed when it wants, but when it has received a commandment from God. A human being is not in good health whenever he wants, but when his Creator gives the order. It is not when you want

---

[26] The text has been restored; A omits 'sun' (*šmš*), and B omits 'heaven' (*šmy'*).

that you catch a wild animal, but when this has been granted to you. The emperor does not win in battles with (enemy) peoples when he wants, nor does the emperor reign when he wants, but when the Lord has given him imperial authority.[27] [VIII] We should recognize, acknowledge and worship Christ who said "I bring to death and I bring to life".'[28]

36. Africanus said, 'Who then is he who has authority over all these things, whom you say is a crucified god?'

37. Phokas said, 'If it is not because you have heard of His Passion, while you fail to consider His might and His resurrection,[29] whence is it that you call Him "crucified" - for this too is something great. And if you want to know, take the Spirit's books and recognize who is your Creator and the Fashioner of (the emperor) whom you call "ruler of the world". In this way you will realize who is God and His Son Jesus Christ who was crucified.'

38. Africanus said, 'Your discourse that I have listened to is very alluring - I don't suppose even Demosthenes[30] (could have) thought up all this! But for now, consent and agree to sacrifice; otherwise you will force me to put you to death - for I shall put you to death (using) harsh punishments and fire. If I do not (do so), I am aware that there are more than fifty thousand people living in these regions whom you will turn away from offering sacrifice.'

39. [IX] Phokas said, 'How much more important that I should die rather than the entire world perish because of my transgression. Rather, it is with great joy that I approach the fire,

---

[27] The passage from 'The clouds...authority' is absent from the Greek, but is present in the Armenian.

[28] Cf. I Sam. 2:6, and compare 2 Kgs 5:7. In the Greek the words are attributed to 'God speaking through the prophet', not 'Christ' (the Armenian just has 'God').

[29] B 'His love'.

[30] The name is badly corrupted in A.

lest, because of one sheep, the entire flock be (found) with blemish. For these are the commands and promises which I have received from our Lord Jesus Christ.'

40. Africanus said, 'I am greatly grieved for you, and I have pity on you, as on an educated and renowned person, but here you are experienced[31] in standing up against my orders.'

41. Phokas said, 'You should not wish to destroy me causing yourself grief. All your threats and (torture-)combs are despicable in my eyes, and they are considered nothing. From now on bring along and carry out what you are wanting to do, for you are not able to have control over my words, nor over my state of mind, for my custom is to be with the Lord, and my confession is in Him: these in my eyes are professions (better) than ten thousands of people like Demosthenes.'[32]

42. Africanus said, 'If you had been advanced in years, I would have said[33] that you had become feeble-minded; and if you had needed (this), I would have said that this is why you wanted to die.'

43. Phokas said, 'I am escaping from all sorts of money, wealth and possessions in order to acquire a single pearl[34] which neither you, nor he who rules over you, is able to take away from me. So if you want, torture me and lacerate me, for I am not going to sacrifice to idols.'

44. Africanus said, 'It is to the pure and blameless gods that we are sacrificing, whereas are you saying that they are defiled?'

45. Phokas said, 'It is not just (the case) that they are defiled, haughty, sorcerers, adulterers, sacrilegious and lifeless de-

---

[31] = B (*mtns' 'nt*); A 'hated' (*mstnyt*).
[32] Paragraphs 40 and 41 are absent from the Greek (but present in the Armenian).
[33] B omits 'I would have said'.
[34] Cf. Mt.13:46.

mons, but so (are) also those who speak of any (deity) apart from the one exalted God almighty, to whom glory and honour is ascribed through our Lord Jesus Christ, for eternal ages, amen.'

46. [X] When a considerable number of the brethren had sealed (his words) by saying 'Amen', there was suddenly a sound of mighty waters,[35] and as if from the force of a mighty earthquake[36] Africanus too fell down, reduced to silence on the ground like a corpse, along with all the troops around him, at these things that they saw, and at what Christ wished to manifest, (there being) a great flash of light from the sky, ten times[37] (stronger) than the sun, and three angels appeared, riding mounts of fire. Great fright and terror fell upon us, and we all stood there in amazement. (The angels) greeted the blessed Phokas and (then) were raised up to heaven.

47. A half hour after these things occurred, Terentina, the wife of Africanus, ran up, her hair loose and her head dishevelled, along with her five children and all her maidservants: she fell down before Phokas, beseeching him saying, 'Give me (back) my husband, and I and all my household will believe in God' - (a promise) which she indeed carried out.[38]

48. Then the blessed Phokas summoned all the clergy and prayed over him.[39] Afterwards, delivered by the miracle, (Africanus) departed and sent (message) to the emperor concerning the renowned might of our Lord and concerning the hope of the Christians.

49. [XI] Then the emperor Trajan sent for the blessed Phokas

---

[35] Cf. Ps. 93(92):4.

[36] = B Greek, Armenian; A 'sound'.

[37] B 'ten thousand times' (*'pyn* > *'lpyn*).

[38] The intervention of Africanus' wife was perhaps modelled on that of Pilate's wife in Mt. 27:19.

[39] Sc. Africanus.

and said to him, 'Are you that Phokas who did not recognize the might of our rule? And why do you not recognize[40] my orders? In what do you trust? What God do you revere? But I do not imagine that an age such as yours requires any advisers,[41] and you should be advising yourself, but I advise you not to despise my orders.[42] For if it is of your own doing that you are not in your (right) mind, (then) you should regain your senses: by means of many tortures you shall realize who Trajan is, and who is the one whom you honour and serve.'

50. Phokas said to him, 'Is it permitted to speak in your presence, O emperor? If so, I will cause this sea in front of me to retreat back at speed.'

51. Trajan said, 'You are permitted to speak, especially if it is something beneficial.'

52. Phokas said, 'The beginning of your reign was given by God.[43] Do you recognize the one who gave it to you?'

53. Trajan said, 'My reign was given to me by the many gods - to whom one ought to sacrifice. It is obligatory for us to accord honour to those who save us; for this reason we ought to offer sacrifice for our[44] lives.'

54. Phokas said, 'It is right, O emperor, that we should obey God almighty and keep His commandments. We should be subject also to leaders and obey those who (live) by an upright religion, and not those with a sinful one.'

55. Trajan said, 'Were you summoned to sacrifice, or to do philosophy?'

56. Phokas said, 'To whom do I have to sacrifice?'

---

[40] B 'obey'.
[41] = B (*mlwk*) Greek; A 'promises' (*mwlkn*).
[42] B 'the orders of my kingdom'.
[43] = B Greek; A 'Who gave you the beginning of your reign?'
[44] A and B have 'their', clearly a corruption.

57. Trajan said, 'To Asklepiades.'[45]

58. Phokas said, 'Where is your god, so that I can see him?'

59. [XII] When he and Trajan had come to the temple, (Trajan) told him, 'Here are the gods of the whole earth, who guard its inhabitants.'

60. Phokas said to one of the sculpted (figures), 'I'm speaking to you, stone; do you want to eat and drink? Do you want to put on some clothes? Do you want to smell something? Are you desiring a sacrifice? Look, O emperor, at how useless your[46] gods are: those that are standing do not sit down, and those that are seated do not stand up. Their mouth may be open, but they do not speak. We have cried out to them, but they do not hear. Their eyes do not observe (anything); they do not take hold[47] of a sacrifice with their hands. Would you like me to cast one of them (down)? It will not speak or complain, or be upset; it will not cry out to the emperor to help it. Whereas if some human being should invoke (the emperor), his cause will be seen to. How can it save anyone? See what these (objects) are that you honour, O emperor.'

61. Trajan said, 'You astonish my mind, Phokas. If you were a sailor, wouldn't you hold Poseidon in honour?'

62. Phokas said, 'I was a sailor, O emperor, and a steersman - and I was guided by the Lord of all; and I offer the sacrifice that I was instructed (to offer).'

63. [XIII] Trajan said, 'Let us too see to whom you are sacrificing, and what it is that you are offering to him.'

---

[45] 'Asclepius' in the Greek and Armenian. This provides a possible link with Asterius's Homily (IV.13.2): 'Let the places of healing be idle; let Asclepius no more be venerated'.

[46] mss 'our' (by an easy corruption).

[47] B 'try out'.

64. Phokas said, 'It is not possible for you to know, for it is written, "You shall not cast your pearls in front of swine".'[48]

65. Trajan said, 'So we are swine, according to what you are saying?'

66. Phokas said, 'Would that you were dumb animals; then you would not be guilty at the judgement for sacrificing to stones - which are not worthy even of the term 'dumb animals'.[49] For what is better and more excellent? You who hold such great authority, or those (idols) who do not even give an answer to what is addressed to them?'

67. Trajan said, 'I will give orders for you to be suspended on a piece of wood. Let us see what help this empty cleverness of yours provides for you!'

68. Phokas said, 'I am ready to be suspended on wood - and I shall (then) be in the air, in the direction of heaven, with my Lord, whereas you and your gods will go down to Sheol below, and proceed to outer darkness. Then you will see what is the power of the heavenly God!'

69. [XIV] While he was being combed on all his members, he refused to deny, and did not utter a word, though his lips moved as he prayed.

70. When he had sealed (his prayer) and said 'Amen', there was a great groan from heaven, and a voice was heard saying, 'Be courageous, Phokas, for I am with you; a place in Paradise has been prepared for you, along with all the leaders and fathers who have not denied me and my Father. But now Trajan is going to the place you spoke of: and he[50] will receive the judgement prepared for him, which is unending.'

---

[48] Mt. 7:6.

[49] = B (cf. Greek); A has '(you) who are not worthy of the term "human beings"'.

[50] Both mss have 'you', evidently misconstruing the Greek.

71. As fear settled on Trajan, he gave the order to take (Phokas) down, and instructed four soldiers to guard him, as well as one centurion whose name was Crispinus.[51] These took him off[52] and transferred him to the prison - while (all the time) he was praising and magnifying the Lord. They were guarding him with great vigilance, he being in the stocks. They closed the door firmly, and were diligently on watch outside.

72. [XV] In the middle of the night he was praying as follows: 'May Jesus hear, Son of God, our Lord, the Holy Name, Name that is from eternity God; God of the angels, God of every name that is named,[53] Shepherd of the rational sheep, guard Your sheep so that they are not plundered; chase away from them the many-footed wolf, the deceiver and plunderer; may he not be given any place in the labour[54] of Your hands. Let the Befouled One not render unclean[55] Your vineyard, which is a plantation of gold; let him not defile Your dove that is without blemish. May that serpent full of scars not render Your servants unclean, he being befouled and destructive. Rather, preserve Your sheep and the vine that Your right hand has planted,[56] Your very same[57] sheep whom You have acquired with Your most precious blood.[58] Do not give Your Ark over to those in

---

[51] B 'Carpianus'; Greek 'Priscus', with variants 'Crispinus' and 'Crispianus'. He is left unnamed in the Armenian.

[52] = B; A 'down' (a single letter's difference).

[53] Cf. Eph. 1:21.

[54] = B (*ml*); A 'entry' (*m'ln*).

[55] B 'reach' (*nmṭ* < *nṭm*) (and again further on).

[56] Cf. Ps. 80(79):15. The passage from 'Let the Befouled One....planted' is absent from the Greek, but is present in the Armenian (in a somewhat different form).

[57] Thus by a small correction (reading *lah* instead of *la*) to A's text.

[58] B 'bought at a great price with Your blood' (cf. Rev.5:9)

TRANSLATION

error, so that it goes astray,[59] for You are its Helmsman (lit: sailor).[60]

73. 'I thank You, Lord Jesus Christ, and I praise and thank Your Father as I supplicate and beseech You to be with me today in the feast, for I have come spotless to Your Bridal Chamber[61] today. Do not reject me who comes to You today.[62] Preserve my soul, as a father, and as God, and as a shepherd, lest the serpent drag me off: let his feet not be raised or lifted up over me. Neither with gold nor with silver has he persuaded me to lose the precious pearl.[63] But see how I am leaving everything behind so as to acquire for You a precious flock, (for You,) the greatly merciful Lord most high. Bring me close to Your Father and raise me up to the gate of Your royal palace. For in Your hands is the glory of Your great Father, along with the Holy Spirit for ever.'

74. [XVI] When he had completed his prayer the prison opened. There were a thousand[64] candles in that well-guarded place. The soldiers hastily leapt up from their places and fell at his feet, asking of him that they should receive holy baptism. He led them off and went to the seashore, outside the city, and he gave them the 'seal' of Christ. The Lord was also seen by them, and they departed and were

---

[59] B 'to erasure...so that it is erased' (reading forms from the root *ṭ'*, rather than *t'*).

[60] The last sentence is absent from the Greek, but present in the Armenian.

[61] The Greek has *pastos*; for the widespread use of *gnona* in Syriac see my 'The Bridal Chamber of Light: a distinctive feature of the Syriac liturgical tradition', *The Harp* 18 (2005), 179–91.

[62] B om. 'today'.

[63] Cf Mt. 13:46.

[64] = B (*'lp*); cf. Greek 'ten thousand'. A by an easy corruption has 'not even (any)' (*'pl*).

filled as it were with the entire Law; and we[65] entered the prison.

75. In the morning, when great crowds came to the market, expecting to see the contest of the holy Phokas, once he had been summoned before Trajan's tribunal, Trajan said to him, 'Sacrifice to Poseidon.'

76. Phokas said, 'I am not going to sacrifice to devils.[66] You do not recognize who it is who has given you this authority. Is it not right for me to say that you are dumb beasts who do not recognize God Your benefactor?'

77. Trajan said, 'Sacrifice to your god.'

78. Phokas said, 'My God does not need anything, apart from thanksgiving,[67] as well as fasting and a pure heart. Everything that exists is the work of His hands, and He provides for all that is and for all that shall be.'

79. [XVII] Trajan said, 'As the beginning of your philosophy, sacrifice to the gods, for a crucified god does not exist.'

80. Phokas said, 'You heard the voice of your 'crucified one', and you shook, and your hair stood on end. If He is incited against you, who is able to stand before Him? For His threat melts mountains[68] and His wrath burns up seas.'[69]

81. Trajan said, 'Don't you realize with whom you are speaking[70] and with whom you are dealing?'

82. Phokas said, 'Because I know with whom I am dealing, I

---

[65] So also Armenian; Greek 'they'. For another 'we' passage, see 46. For the episode of 74, compare Acts 16:25–33.

[66] The Greek (cf. Armenian) adds here: 'Trajan said "Are the gods demons and are we swine? Who, then, is the god?" Phokas said'. This will have fallen out of the Syriac through homoioteleuton at some stage.

[67] = B, Greek, Armenian; A + 'and love'.

[68] Cf. Ps. 97(96):5.

[69] Perhaps cf. Is. 50:2. The Greek verb, however, is *rhēssei*, perhaps reflecting Exod. 14:16.

[70] = B; A has lost a phrase through homoioteleuton.

am not going to sacrifice. But you will not hear anything else from me: this I acknowledge in your presence, that I am a Christian.'

83. Trajan said, 'I give orders for you to be thrown into unquenchable lime. Let us see if your God will save you!'

84. When they had cast him (into the lime pit) for a space of three hours, they raised him up unharmed, just as he was the moment he fell in.

85. [XVIII] Trajan said, 'Because of you, the baths have been heated up for three days, without being opened for three days. I order that you be thrown in there!'

86. The holy Phokas made the sign of his Lord's cross and entered the bathhouse. The bathhouse was glowing like bronze from the fire. As he stood there in the midst he began to bless and say, 'I give thanks to You, O Lord, that You have held me worthy of bonds and fetters in prison, and of lacerations and many trials; and today, O Lord, send Your angel and deliver me from the hands of Trajan, lest the gentiles should say, "Where is his God?".'[71]

87. When he had completed his prayer, he raised up his final praise with an Amen. He gave up his soul at sunset. Trajan ordered the baths to be opened, and the remains of the blessed Phokas were found to be like beautiful nard and like crystal, like a precious incense - while the bathhouse was found to be as though it had never been heated.

88. [XIX] When Trajan saw the remains of the blessed Phokas, he cried out and said to his soldiers, 'Look at the perseverance of this man and his faith. Truly there is no other God but "He who dwells in the heaven"'.[72] And he was (filled) with fright and trembling.

---

[71] Ps. 79(78):10.
[72] See note to 7.

89. He went out from the bathhouse and the holy Phokas appeared to him[73] at the door, saying to him, 'Trajan, you tyrant, go to the place prepared for you, to the bottommost depth, to the everlasting fire. For me the Paradise of delight has been opened up, but for you Sheol is opened up - for you and your shades[74] there shall be no patience granted to you, apart from three days, seeing that you have shed the blood of many righteous people.'

90. Trajan went to his palace rigid with a fever, and he fell onto his bed. Eaten up by worms,[75] his soul left him.

91. [XX] This is the contest and the life of the holy Phokas. He was the first to be a martyr in Pontus, and he is spoken of up to this day - and (he will be) for ever. A sailor and pilot of the ships of those who travel by sea, he is renowned all over the world, along with his martyrdom and struggles: he is to be found in the high country of Armenia, of Pontus, and of Paphlagonia.[76] (He was) a man on the rank of the Apostles, who was numbered among the saints, and who received the crown of victory from the Lord, to whom be praise and authority along with the Holy Spirit, for eternal ages, amen.

Ended is the martyrdom of bishop Phokas.

---

[73] Lit. 'was revealed over him', a usage not uncommonly found in early Syriac texts which goes back to the Palestinian Targum: see my 'A Palestinian Targum feature in Syriac', *Journal of Jewish Studies* 46 (1995), 271–82.

[74] Representing Greek *eidōlois*; B has 'your error' *ṭ'wtk* < *ṭlnytk*).

[75] Cf. Acts 12:23 (Herod).

[76] Thus also the Armenian; the Greek omits 'of Pontus and of Paphlagonia'.

Syriac Text

Syriac text   A: Vatican Syr. 160, ff.205r.1–210r.2
                  B: Vatican Syr. 160, ff.224v.1–231v.1.

The text is that of A, unless otherwise stated; variant readings of B are given in the apparatus.

[Syriac text]

---

[118] ܡܫܘܕܥܘܬܗ
[119] om.
[120] ܘܡܟܘܠܐ
[121] om. sey.
[122] ܐܝܟ

35

A 205r.2
B 224v.2

B 225r.1

A 205v.1

---

¹²³ ܠܩܘܡܗ

¹²⁴ ܡܒܛܠܝܢ

¹²⁵ = B; A + sey.

¹²⁶ ܨܒܘܬܐ

¹²⁷ ܘܐܪ

¹²⁸ ܘܒܥܝܢ +

¹²⁹ A verb such as <ܐܡܪ> must have fallen out.

¹³⁰ ܣܘܝܘܗܝ,

¹³¹ ܐܢܫ +

¹³² om.

¹³³ ܕܠܗ +

ܘܓܙ̈ܪܝ ܕܝܢܐ ܠܐ ܗܘܐ ܡܢ ܒܠܚܘܕ ܡܕܝܢܐ
ܗܘܬ ܘܡܕܒܪܢܐ [134] ܠܥܡ̈ܡܐ.

3. ܕܘܒܪܐ ܕܝܢ ܕܫܩ̈ܘܗܝ ܕܛܘܒܢܐ ܦܘܡܐ ܐܝܬܘܗܝ
ܗܢܐ. ܟܕ ܛܠܐ ܗܘܐ [135] ܐܫܬܪܒ ܡܢ ܚܘܒܐ
ܡܕܒܪܢܐ. ܐܠܐ ܕܚܝܐ ܘܕܠܐ ܡܘܡ ܐܝܟ ܗܢܐ
ܕܗܪܝ ܡܢ ܛܠܝܘܬܗ ܥܡܠ ܢܦܫܗ ܥܠ ܚܣ̈ܦܬܗ
ܒܫܠܬܐ. ܘ ܓܒܪܐ ܢܝܚܐ ܗܘܐ ܝܨܪ ܥܠ ܐܚܐ.
ܒܠܒܒܐ ܠܫܘ̈ܬܦܐ [136]. ܟܕ ܐܝܬܘܗܝ ܡܕܒܪܢܐ
ܒܬܪܐܝܬ [137]. ܟܕ ܡܟܝܟ ܘܡܬܪܬܐ ܠܟܠ ܐܢܫ
ܐܝܟ ܕܙܕܩ ܘܢܟܦ. ܘܥܡ ܟܠ ܐܢܫ ܠܐ ܗܘܐ.
ܗܠܟ ܕܝܢ ܕܢܫ̈ܩܘܗܝ ܐܘ ܓܒܘ̈ܗܝ ܠܐ | ܐܢܫ B 225r.2
ܡܨܐ ܡܢ ܒܢ̈ܝ ܐܢܫܐ ܕܢܬܘܒ ܐܢܫ ܐܝܟ ܗܘ
ܕܐܝܬܘܗܝ: ܒܦܫܝܩܘܬܐ ܕܝܢ ܗܐ [138] ܐܘܕܒܒܘܗܝ.

4. ܟܕ ܓܙܪ ܐܬܚܠܦܘ ܡܣܟ̈ܢܐ ܡܢ ܓܘܪܐ
ܕܒܣ̈ܦܠܝܐ. ܐܦܝܣܩܘܦܐ ܡܕܒܪܢܐ ܠܗܢܐ ܐܝܟ
ܕܠܐܦܐ [139] ܣܝܥܬܐ ܕܟܗ̈ܢܐ ܡܬܒܪܝܢ ܗܘܐ
ܘܟܠܗ ܗܘܐ ܠܗ. ܟܕ ܢܣܒܘܗܝ ܘܒܬܪ ܓܢܣܗ | A 205v.2
ܘܗܢܐ ܡܟܝܟ ܗܘܐ ܒܬܪ ܡܗܝܡܢܐ ܕܙܪ̈ܝܐ
ܘܪܥܝܐ ܫܦܝܐ.

5. ܘܟܕ ܐܬܐ ܩܕܡ ܒܝܫܐ ܐܦܝܣܩܘܦܐ ܡܦܪܟܐ
ܐܡܪ ܗܘ ܦܘܡܐ ܗܘ ܕܐܡܪ ܕܠܝܬ [140] ܐܠܗ̈ܐ.
ܘܠܐܢܫ ܥܠ ܦܪܘܣܐ ܠܐ ܡܕܪܐ ܕܐܠܗܐ ܗܘ.
ܐܡܪ ܠܝ. ܠܐ ܗܐ ܥܠ ܒܠܥܕ̈ܝܐ ܡܢ ܐܝܬܘܗܝ
ܐܒܘ. ܡܢܘ ܐܚܪܝܢ ܐܠܗܐ ܐܝܬ.

6. ܦܘܡܐ ܕܝܢ ܡܟܝܟ ܗܘܐ ܘܫܬܩ. ܐܦܝܣܩܘܦܐ
ܐܡܪ ܠܗ. ܠܐ ܐܡܪܬ ܘܡܗܝܡܢܬ ܦܬܓܡܐ ܥܠ
ܡܕܡ ܕܐܬܐܡܪ. ܐܘ ܠܐ ܝܕܥ ܐܢܬ ܐܝܟܐ
ܡܟܝܟ ܐܢܬ.

---

134 + ܡܕܒܪܢܐ

135 A negative must have fallen out; perhaps the text once read ܟܕ ܛܠܐ ܠܐ

136 om. sey.

137 = B; A ܒܬܪܝܐܝܬ

138 = B; A ܗܢܐ

139 = B; A ܕܠܩܘܒܠܬܐ

140 ܕܠܐ ܐܝܬ

38   THE MARTYRDOM OF ST PHOKAS

7. ܗܘܐ ܐܡܪ ܠܗ ܐܢ ܗܟܠ ܐܠܗܐ ܐܝܬܘܗܝ ܗܘܐ B 225v.1
| ܐܒܘܗܝ ܕܩܐܣܪ ܕܡܠܟܐ ܗܘܐ 141 ܐܢ ܕܝܢ
ܠܕ ܒܪ ܐܢܫܐ ܐܝܬܘܗܝ ܐܝܟܢܐ ܗܘܐ ܠܗ ܒܪܗ ܕܟܠܝܘܗܝ
ܕܙܪܥܗ ܡܢ ܟܠ ܥܠܡܐ ܗܘ.

8. ܐܝܣܘܕܪܘܣ ܐܡܪ ܠܗ. ܠܐ ܐܬܘܟܕ ܐܢܘܢ ܒܪܝ،   A 208r.1
ܐܠܗܐ ܐܚܪܢܐ.

9. ܗܘܐ ܐܡܪ ܠܗ. ܐܠܐ ܓܝܪ ܗܘܐ ܠܗ ܠܩܐܣܪ
ܚܒܠܬܐ ܡܬܒܪܝܢܘܬܐ. ܐܠܐ ܡܟܐ|ܐܘ ܐܝܟ ܕܡܝ ܕܝܢ
ܠܕ ܥܠܠܬܐ ܗܘ ܥܠ ܗܕܐ ܕܗܒܬ ܠܗ
ܫܡܐ.

10. ܐܝܣܘܕܪܘܣ ܐܡܪ ܠܗ. ܡܢ ܗܘ ܗܟܠ ܒܪ ܚܐܪ̈ܝܢܘܗܝ
ܐܝܟ ܕܐܠܗܐ.

11. ܗܘܐ ܐܡܪ ܠܗ ܡܢ ܗܢܐ ܕܟܠ ܟܢܫܐ ܕܐܪܥܐ   B 225v.2
ܐܣܬ. ܐܝܟ ܓܝܪ ܗܘ ܕܒܪܐ ܠܫܡܝܐ ܘܠܐܪܥܐ
ܕܡܣܘܒܠ ܫܡܫܐ ܘܣܗܪܐ ܘܡܟܒܕܝܢ ܘܢܘܟܒܐ
ܕܟܠ ܐܠܗܐ ܐܝܬܝܗܝ ܢܚ ܐܝܟ ܕܐܢܬ.
ܘܕܝܒܐ ܟܠܗ ܟܐܒܐ ܠܘܬܗܘܢ ܘܡܐܟܘܠܬܐ ܠܐܠܗܐ
ܠܐ ܕܕܚܠܬ ܚܛܐ ܒܪܐ ܕܝܘܡܢ ܗܘܐ
ܫܡܐ ܐܬܚܙܝ ܒܝܢܘܗܝ |.

12. ܐܝܣܘܕܪܘܣ ܐܡܪ. ܐܝܟܘ ܡܠܬܗ ܛܒܗ ܗܘܐ
ܠܐ ܐܝܟ ܠܟܠܗܘܢ، ܕܐܢܬ ܠܕ.

13. ܗܘܐ ܐܡܪ ܠܗ ܐܝܟ ܕܐܠܗܐ ܐܠܐ
ܐܝܟ ܕܐܡܪܝ ܚܝ̈ܐ ܕܐܠܗܐ. ܠܗ ܓܝܪ
ܠܒܠܥܕܘܗܝ ܐܠܐ ܡܝܬ ܐܠܐ ܠܐ ܐܬܒܪܝ   A 208r.2
ܠܐ ܐܫܬܟܚ ܗܘܐ ܕܐܠܗܐ، ܐܘ ܓܝܪ ܗܘ ܚܫ |.
ܐܝܟ ܕܐܡܪ ܐܝܬܘܗܝ ܐܝܬܐ ܕܐܠܗܐ ܐܢܬ، ܐܠܐ
ܐܝܟ ܪܢܐ143 ܕܬܢܢ ܬܠܠܬܐ144 ܚܣܦܢܝ ܠܝ.
ܐܘ ܕܐܠܬ ܒܐ ܓܝܪ ܐܝܬܐ ܐܬܡܣܪܚ ܕܒܘܗܝ

---

141 ܡܗܠܝ
142 cj; A B ܗܠܐ
143 = B; A ܕܐܢܝ
144 = B; A ܬܠܝܠܬܐ

TEXT   39

16. ܘܐܡܪ̈ܗܘܢ ܐܡܪ ܡܪܢ ܠܢ ܐܝܟܢ | ܐܝܟ ܕܐܡܪܬ¹⁴⁸ B 226r.1
17. ܘܐܡܪ ܡܪܢ ܐܡܪ ܐܢܐ ܠܟܘܢ ܗܘܐ ܒܗ ܡܢ ܝܘܡܐ ܩܕܡܝܐ ܕܠܐ ܝܕܥܬܐ ܘܡܚܘܬܐ. ܐܠܐ ܒܐܝܕܗ ܠܐ ܗܘܬ ܒܪܫܝܬ. ܒܗ ¹⁴⁹ܐܝܟ ܐܝܟܐ ܕܠܐ ܡܫܬܟܚ ܐܢܬ ܬܡܢ. ܡܢ ܗ̇ܘ ܒܥܕܢܐ ܠܐ ܡܫܬܟܚ ¹⁵⁰ܗܘܐ ܒܗ̇. ܐܪܐ ܐܝܟܢ ܡܫܬܟܚ ܗܘ ܗܫܐ ܒܐܝܬܘܬܐ ܘܡܫܬܟܚ ܐܢܐ ܒܐܝܬܘܬܗ. ܘܗܟܘܬ ܒܐܝܕܗ ¹⁵¹ܡܫܬܟܚ | ܐܝܬ ܗ̣ܘ܀ ܘܡܫܬܟܚܐ ܐܠܟܘܢ A 208v.1 ܐܝܟ ܐܢ̇ܐ ¹⁵²ܡܫܘܕܥܬܐ ܚܕܐ ܕܬܘܒ ܠܐ ܐܢܬ ܡܬܠܒܠ ܐܠܦܐ.

---

¹⁴⁷ = B; A ܡܓܝܢܐ
¹⁴⁸ = B; A ܕܐܡܪܬ
¹⁵⁰ = B; A ܡܫܬܟܚ ܗܘܐ
¹⁵¹ + sey.
¹⁵² om. sey.
¹⁵⁴ = B; A ܐܠܐ ܐܢ
¹⁵⁵ om. ܐܠ
¹⁵⁶ om.

40 THE MARTYRDOM OF ST PHOKAS

[Syriac text, sections 20–25, not transliterated]

---

157 ܡܛܠܬܐ
158 ܕܚܙܘ
159 cj; A B ܐܠܐ
160 (ܕܒܝܬ =) ܕܚܒܝܬ
161 ܘܠܐ
162 om.
163 = B; A ܕܐܢ
164 om. *waw*

TEXT 41

A 206r.1

26.

27.

28.

29. B 226v.2

30.

31.

A 206r.2

32.

---

¹⁶⁵ ܘܣܝܡܬܐ ܘܨܠܘܬܐ
¹⁶⁶ om. sey.
¹⁶⁷ = B; A ܘܒܪܬܐ
¹⁶⁸ = B; A omits though homoioteleuton from ܐܢܬ in 28 to here; a second hand later crossed out 29, due to the confusion of speakers that had arisen.
¹⁶⁹ ܘܡܫܒܚܬܐ

34. |
 |
 | ,
---

172 cj ; A ; B
175 = B; A

36. ܐܦܪܘܣܝܘܣ ܐܡܪ ܡܢܘ ܗܟܝܠ ܐܝܬܘܗܝ، ܗܘ ܕܥܠ
ܟܠܗܝܢ ܡܫܠܛ ܗܘ ܕܐܡܪܬ ܕܐܠܗܐ ܗܘ[177]
ܘܙܕܝܩܐ.

37. ܦܘܠܐ ܐܡܪ. ܘܐܢ ܕܝܢ ܠܐ ܐܢܬ ܓܝܪ
ܒܫܡܗ[178] ܗܘ ܥܒܕܬ. ܒܚܝܠܗ ܕܝܢ ܘܒܚܘܣܢܗ[179]
ܠܐ ܡܬܟܣܐ ܐܢܬ. ܡܢ ܐܝܟܐ ܕܝܢ ܠܟ ܗܕܐ
ܕܬܩܪܘܗܝ، ܘܙܕܝܩܐ ܕܐܦ ܗܕܐ ܪܒܐ. ܘܐܢ ܨܒܝܬ
ܕܬܕܥ ܗܒ ܒܠܒܟ | ܪܘܚܐ ܘܕܥ ܡܢܘ ܒܪܘܚܟ |. A 206v.2
ܘܓܒܠܗ ܕܗܘ ܐܝܟ ܒܠܒܐ[180] ܕܪܘܚܬ ܘܡܢ B 227v.1
ܡܬܬܘܕܥ ܐܢܬ ܡܢܘ ܐܠܗܐ ܐܝܟܐ ܘܒܪܗ ܝܫܘܥ
ܡܫܝܚܐ ܗܘ ܕܐܙܕܩܦ.

38. ܐܦܪܘܣܝܘܣ ܐܡܪ ܗܟܢ ܗܘ ܫܘܕܠܐ ܕܡܟܠܠܢ
ܕܫܒܚܬ. ܒܪܡ ܕܝܢ ܐܦ ܠܐ ܕܡܬܟܣܝܢܘ[181] ܗܠܝܢ
ܟܠܗܝܢ ܐܫܟܚ. ܐܠܐ ܡܟܝܠ ܐܬܦܠܣܦܘ ܘܕܝܢ
ܕܬܕܥ ܕܠܐ ܬܐܠܗܝܬ ܐܦܠܛܘܢ[182]. ܕܒܡܚܫܒ
ܒܪܫܐ ܡܫ̈ܝܚܐ ܘܒܢܘܪܐ ܐܦܠܛܘܢ. ܐܠܐ ܢܕܒܬ
ܕܬܬܪ ܡܢ ܣܥܪ ܙ̈ܒܢ ܐܢܫܐ ܡܫܡܢ ܒܗܠܝܢ
ܐܬܘ̈ܬܐ ܕܡܗܦܟܝܢ ܐܢܬ ܠܗܘܢ ܕܠܐ ܢܒܥܘܢ.

39. ܦܘܠܐ ܐܡܪ. ܘܒܗܕܐ ܪܒܐ ܗܕܐ ܕܐܢܐ ܐܡܪܬ
ܐܘ ܗܢܐ ܟܠܗ ܟܠܡܐ ܡܛܠ ܒܪܐ ܦܘܩܕܢ ܢܡܘܣ:
ܐܠܐ ܐܦ ܒܚܕܘܬܐ ܪܒܬܐ ܡܢ ܐܢܐ ܠܘܬ
ܢܘܪܐ ܕܠܐ ܡܛܠ ܚܕ ܒܪܢܫܐ ܒܠܗ ܒܢܐ ܬܗܘܐ
ܒܡܘܡܐ. ܗܠܝܢ ܓܝܪ ܦܘܩ̈ܕܢܐ ܘܡ̈ܠܟܐ ܡܟܠܬ
ܡܢ ܡܪܢ ܝܫܘܥ | ܡܫܝܚܐ. B 227v.2

40. ܐܦܪܘܣܝܘܣ ܐܡܪ ܐܢܐ ܟܠܗܝܢ ܗܘ ܗܟܢ ܒܫܘܠܐ
ܠܝ ܘܫܡܥܬ ܐܢܐ ܟܠܗܝܢ. ܐܝܟ | ܕܥܠ ܙܕܩܐ A 207r.1
ܘܓܒܪܐ ܡܫܡܗܐ. ܐܢܬ ܓܝܪ ܗܐ ܡܬܚܙܝܐ[183]
ܐܢܬ ܕܬܩܘܡ ܠܘܩܒܠ ܦܘܩܕܢ.

---

177 om.

178 ܫܡܗ

179 ܘܒܚܘܣܗ

180 + sey.

181 = B; A ! ܕܡܬܟܣܝܬ

182 ܕܐܦܠܛ ܒܡܚܫܒ

183 = B; A ܡܬܚܙܐ

41. ܦܘܩܐ ܐܡܪ ܠܗ ܒܪ ܡܚܝܡ ܐܢܬ ܢܦܫܟ ܬܓܪܐ
ܕܬܘܒܢܝܢ. ܟܠܗܘܢ ܓܝܪ ܠܡܫܚܝܢ ܘܫܘܦܝܢ
ܒܥܝܢ ܐܢܘܢ ܡܕܡ. ܘܠܐ ܢܫܟܚܝܢ ܠܗ. ܡܚܝܠ ܡܕܡ
ܕܬܓܪܐ ܐܢܬ[184] ܕܐܬܡܟܪܬ ܡܟܘܪ. ܠܐ ܓܝܪ ܟܠ
ܡܠܬܝ، ܡܬܓܪܐ ܐܢܬ ܕܐܬܬܫܠܠܬ. ܐܦ ܠܐ ܠܟܠ
ܡܫܡܫ ܒܪܚܡܘ. ܚܙܝ، ܓܝܪ ܕܒܡ ܡܪܢܐ. ܘܬܬܕܟܪ،
ܕܒܗ. ܡܢ ܙܒܢܬܗ ܕܐܝܟ ܕܡܫܬܡܠܘܢ[185] ܐܘܩܝܢ
ܐܢܘܢ ܒܚܢܘ.

42. ܐܦܪܝܩܘܣ ܐܡܪ. ܐܝܠܐ ܡܫܟܚ ܗܘܝܬ ܐܡܪ
ܗܘܝܬ[186] ܕܫܬܘܪܬ[187] ܠܟ. ܘܐܝܟܐ ܫܟܝܚܐ ܗܘܝܬ
ܐܡܪ ܗܘܝܬ ܕܡܠܠ ܗܘܐ[188] ܓܒܠܬ ܕܐܬܓܒܠܬ.

43. ܦܘܩܐ ܐܡܪ ܡܢ ܟܠ ܢܦܫܝ ܘܡܢ ܟܠ ܒܬܘܡܝ.
ܘܡܢ ܟܠ ܚܝܠ ܡܚܫܒܬܐ | ܐܢܐ ܗܘ. ܕܫܪܪܐ B 228r.1
ܡܢ ܓܒܠܬܐ ܐܝܠܐ. ܐܢܫܐ[189] ܕܠܐ ܐܢܬ ܘܠܐ
ܗܘ ܕܡܟܠܝܢ ܟܠܗܝܢ ܡܬܓܪܐ ܕܢܦܫ[190] ܡܢܝ. ܐܢ
[191] ܓܒܠܬ ܡܚܝܠ ܐܫܬܕܪ ܒܪ ܘܫܘܪܝܢ ܕܠܐ
ܡܕܒܪ ܐܢܐ ܠܬܘܒܬܐ. | A 207r.2

44. ܐܦܪܝܩܘܣ ܐܡܪ ܠܕܒܪܐ ܘܕܠܐ ܙܢܝܐ ܐܠܗܐ[192]
ܐܝܟ ܡܕܒܪ ܐܝܟ ܘܐܢܬ ܡܫܡܫܢܐ ܐܡܪ
ܐܢܬ ܕܐܠܗܘܬܗܘܢ.

45. ܦܘܩܐ ܐܡܪ ܠܗ[193] ܠܘ ܗܢܘܢ ܒܠܚܘܕ
ܐܠܗܘܬܗܘܢ ܡܫܡܫܢܐ ܘܫܪܪܐ ܘܚܘܒܐ ܘܓܢܝܐ
ܘܡܫܠܡܝ، ܒܗܬ ܐܠܗܐ ܘܕܝܢܐ ܕܠܐ ܢܦܫ
ܐܠܗܘܬܗܘܢ ܐܠܐ ܐܦ ܗܢܘܢ ܕܐܡܪܝܢ ܠܒܪ ܡܢ
ܗܘ ܚܕ ܐܠܗܐ ܡܠܟܐ ܘܐܚܕ ܟܠ ܗܘ ܕܠܗ
ܫܘܒܚܐ ܘܐܝܩܪܐ ܡܫܬܪܝܪ ܒܚܕ ܡܢܝ ܢܦܫܝ

184 ܬܘܒ +
185 ܕܡܫܬܡܠܝܢ
186 om. ܗܘܝܬ ܐܡܪ
187 ܕܫܬܘܪܬ
188 ܗܕܐ
189 = B; A ܐܝܢܐ
190 ܕܢܦܫܗ
191 ܘܠܐ
192 om. sey.!
193 om.

 | B 228r.2
 | A 207v.1
 | B 228v.1
---
[195] = B; A
[197] = B; A
[199] = B; A

ܬܚܒܠ ܐܢܬ. ܡܢ ܐܝܢܐ ܐܠܗܐ ܕܝܠ ܐܢܬ. ܒܪܡ
ܕܝܢ ܠܐ ܫܒܪ ܐܢܐ ܕܫܘܡܬܐ ܕܐܝܟ ܗܕܐ
ܫܘܡܐ ܟܠ ܡܠܟ̈ܐ[202] ܐܠܐ ܠܢܦܫܟ ܡܠܟ
ܐܢܬ. | ܘܠܐ ܫܡܥܬ ܦܘܩܕܢܝ[203]. ܐܦ ܓܝܪ ܡܢ A 207v.2
ܙܒܘܬ ܢܦܫܟ[204] ܠܐ ܬܗܘܐ ܙܟܝ[205] ܢܦܫܟ.
ܘܬܚܒܠ ܒܪܚܡܝܟ. ܒܥܒ̈ܕܐ[206] ܡܣܟܢ̈ܐ ܬܒܪ ܕܡܢ
ܐܒܘܬܗܝ ܛܪܝܢܘܣ. ܘܡܢ ܐܒܘܬܗܝ ܗܘ ܕܐܝܬ
ܡܢܛܪ ܐܢܬ[207]. ܘܦܠܚ | ܐܢܬ ܠܗ. B 228v.2

50. ܦܘܩܐ ܐܡܪ ܠܗ ܫܠܝܛ ܠܡܐܡܪ ܡܕܡܝܢ ܐܘ
ܡܠܟܐ ܘܐܦ ܐܒܪܗ[208] ܒܪܗܛܐ ܠܗܢܐ ܡܢܐ
ܕܐܝܬ ܡܕܡ.

51. ܛܪܝܢܘܣ ܐܡܪ ܫܠܝܛ ܠܟ ܠܡܐܡܪ. ܘܬܬܪܐܬ
ܡܕܡ ܕܡܒܝܪ.

52. ܦܘܩܐ ܐܡܪ ܪܥܝܐ ܕܡܠܟܘܬܟ ܡܢ ܐܠܗܐ
ܝܗܒ[209]. ܐܦ ܗܕܐ ܐܢܬ ܠܟܡ ܕܝܗܒ ܠܟ.

53. ܛܪܝܢܘܣ ܐܡܪ ܡܠܟܘܬܝ ܕܝܠܝ ܡܢ ܐܠܗ̈ܐ
ܡܣܟܢ̈ܐ ܝܗܝܒܐ ܠܝ. ܗܢܘܢ ܕܡܬܚܫܒ ܠܗܘܢ
ܠܡܕܒܪܘ. ܐܠܐ ܐܠܝܨܐ ܗܘ ܠܝ ܕܠܡܫܒܚܘܬܗ
ܐܝܟܢܐ ܕܙܕܩ ܢܗܘܐ. ܘܡܛܠ[210] ܗܕܐ ܦܠܐ ܠܝ
ܕܢܕܒܝܪ ܟܠ ܣܢܝ̈ܢ[211].

54. ܦܘܩܐ ܐܡܪ ܕܗܘ ܐܘ ܡܠܟܐ. ܕܠܐܠܗܐ ܐܚܝܕ
ܟܠ ܢܬܚܫܒ ܘܦܘܩ̈ܕܢܘܗܝ[212] ܢܛܪ. ܢܬܚܫܒ ܕܝܢ
ܐܦ ܠܪ̈ܥܝܐ. ܘܢܬܚܫܒ ܠܟܠܗܘܢ ܕܒܕܝܠܬܐ
ܬܫܡܫܬܐ ܗܘܝܢ. ܘܠܐ ܠܟܠܗܘܢ ܕܫܠܛܬܐ ܐܝܟ. | A 209r.1

---

202 = B; A ܡܘܠܟ̈ܢܐ
203 ܠܦܘܩܕܢܐ ܕܡܠܟܘܬܝ
204 ܪܚܡܟ
205 ܗܘܝܟ
206 ܥܒ̈ܕܐ
207 ܠܗ +
208 = B; A ܘܡܢ ܢܒܪܗ
209 = B; A ܡܢ ܝܗܒ ܠܟ
210 ܡܛܠ
211 cj; A B ܣܢܝ̈ܢܗܘܢ
212 ܘܦܘܩ̈ܕܢܘܗܝ

55. ܦܝܪܘܣ ܐܡܪ ܕܬܕܒܚ ܐܬܡܪܬ ܐܘ
ܕܦܝܠܣܘܦܘܬܐ[213] ܬܒܥܐ.

56. B 229r.1 ܦܘܡܐ ܐܡܪ | ܠܡܢ ܐܢܬ ܠܝ ܕܐܕܒܚ.

57. ܦܝܪܘܣ ܐܡܪ ܠܐܣܩܠܦܝܘܣ.

58. ܦܘܡܐ ܐܡܪ ܐܝܟܘ ܐܠܗܢ ܕܐܣܝܘܬܗ.

59. ܟܕ ܕܝܢ ܐܬܐ ܗܘ ܘܦܝܪܘܣ ܠܦܘܡܐ ܐܡܪ ܠܗ.
ܗܐ ܐܠܗܐ ܕܟܠܗ̇[214] ܐܪܥܐ ܕܠܬܚܬܝܗ̇[215]
ܢܛܪ.

60. ܦܘܡܐ ܐܡܪ ܠܚܕ ܡܢ ܟܐܦܐ. ܠܗ ܐܡܪ ܐܢܐ
ܟܐܦܐ. ܝܕܥܬ ܕܬܠܒܫܝܢ ܐܘ ܬܫܬܡ. ܝܕܥܬ
ܕܬܠܒܫܝܢ ܝܕܥܬ ܕܬܪܦܣܝܢ. ܡܛܠ ܕܒܪ ܟܝܬ ܠܕܟܝܐ.
ܣܘܪ ܡܠܟܐ ܕܟܐܦܐ ܐܝܟܢ ܐܠܗܝܢ[216]. ܡܢܗܝܢ
ܘܠܐ[217] ܢܬܟܝܢ ܘܕܢܬܟܝܢ ܠܐ ܡܢܗܝܢ. ܦܘܡܗܘܢ
ܦܬܝܚ ܘܠܐ ܡܡܠܠܝܢ ܡܢܝܢ ܘܠܐ ܥܡܟܝܢ.
ܚܛܝܗܘܢ ܠܐ ܚܣܝܢ ܟܐܢܕܪܗܘܢ ܠܐ ܠܚܡܝܢ[218]
ܕܚܝܬܐ. ܪ ܓܒܐ ܠܝ ܕܐܫܟܪܐ ܚܕ ܡܢܗܘܢ ܘܠܐ
ܢܡܠܠ. ܘܠܐ ܡܬܬܙܝܥ[219] ܘܠܐ ܡܬܚܒܪ. ܘܠܐ
ܦܪܐ ܠܡܠܟܐ ܕܢܒܕܩܗ. ܐܦ ܕܝܢ ܐܝܟ ܡܢ ܒܢܝ
A 209r.2 ܐܢܫܐ ܢܟܝܢ ܡܬܬܟܠܐ | ܢܡܛܬܗ. ܘܐܡܟܢܐ ܠܒܪ
ܐܢܫܐ ܢܫܘܒ ܗܐ ܡܟܢܐ ܐܝܟܢ ܗܠܝܢ ܕܡܛܠ
ܐܝܬ ܡܠܟܐ.

61. B 229r.2 ܦܝܪܘܣ | ܐܡܪ ܐܬܡܪܬܗܝ ܪܒܝܢ ܦܘܡܐ. ܠܐ
ܡܠܟܐ ܗܘܬ ܠܗ ܠܦܘܪܩܢܐ ܡܛܠ ܗܘܬ.

---

213 ܕܦܝܠܘܣܘܦܘܬܐ
214 ܕܠܟܠܗ̇
215 ܘܠܬܚܬܝܗ̇
216 cj; A B ܐܠܗܝܢ
217 ܕܡܢܗܝܢ ܠܐ
218 ܒܣܪܝܢ
219 om. ܘܠܐ ܡܬܬܙܝܥ

ܠܘܩܒܠ ܐܠܐ ܘܠܐ ܡܢ ܥܡ ܕܒܪ | ܠܐ ܫܒܚ
A 209v.1
B 229v.1

---

[221] = B; A (= Peshitta) ܝܬܝܪܐܝܬ
[223] = B; A ܕܗܢܘܢ

TEXT   49

ܘܥܡܥܒܕ ܕܡܐ ܗܝܘܢܐ ܗܘ ܕܘܟܬܐ.   A 209v.2
ܠܢ ܠܐܝܬܘܗܝ | ܐܘܕܥ ܐܝܬܘܗܝ | ܐܢܬ   B 229v.2
ܕܢܫܡܘܢ²³³. ܕܐܣܬܪܝܟ ܕܠܐ. ܐܝܬܝܪܐ ܥܠ ܟܬܒܬܐ   A 210r.1
ܒܠܚܘܕ²³⁵ ܡܬܘܒܘ ܡܕܒܪܗ ܐܣܘܦܐ²³⁴ ܕܡܣܒܪܐ   B 230r.1
ܕܐܝܬܘܗܝ ܡܢܝܬܗ | ܠܒܥܠ ܫܒܥ ܠܐ ܡܕܘܡܐ ܐܠܐ ܐܢܬ |

---

²²⁷ = B; A ܘܐܣܬܢܫ,
²²⁸ = B; A ܐܝܢܝܟܘܬܐ
²³¹ = B; A ܥܒܕܐ!
²³² om. sey.
²³³ = B; A ܕܢܫܡܥ

 |
---

238 cj; A ; B
239 om.
241 om.
243 = B; A
244 om.
246 = B; A

TEXT 51

 | B 230v.1
²⁵¹. | A 210v.1
 | .   B 230v.2

---
²⁵⁰ om. sey.
²⁵¹ om.
²⁵³ = B; A +
²⁵⁵ = B; A om.

82. ܦܘܩܐ ܐܡܪ. ܡܛܠ ܓܒܪ ܕܥܒܕ ܐܢܐ ܥܡ ܡܢܗ
ܐܡܬ ܠܝ. ܠܐ ܡܕܒܚ ܐܢܐ. ܐܠܐ ܡܢ ܠܥܠ ܠܝ
ܐܫܝܢ ܕܢܫܬܡܠܐ[256]. ܗܕܐ ܕܝܢ ܡܘܕܐ | ܐܢܐ A 210v.2
ܡܕܡܝܢ ܕܒܪܘܦܠܝܢܐ ܐܡܬܝ.

83. ܛܪܝܢܘܣ ܐܡܪ ܦܩܕ ܐܢܐ ܘܟܠܫܐ ܕܠܐ ܡܕܒܚܝܢ
ܙܡܢ ܠܝ. ܚܣܝܐ ܐܢ ܦܘܡ ܠܝ ܐܠܗܝ.

84. ܘܟܕ ܐܘܪܒܘܗܝ، ܠܦܘܪܐ ܕܬܠܬ ܥ̈ܫܝܢ ܐܣܩܘܗܝ،
ܕܠܐ ܢܚܫܐ ܐܝܟ ܗܘ ܕܒܗ̇ ܒܥܠܬܐ ܢܦܠ.

85. ܛܪܝܢܘܣ ܐܡܪ ܡܛܠܬܟ ܒܢܐ ܥܒܪܐ[257]. ܗܐ
ܘܗܫܐ ܬܠܬܐ ܐܝܕܐ ܕܠܐ ܐܬܦܬܚܬ ܗܐ
ܬܠܬܐ ܝܘܡ̈ܝܢ. ܬܘܒ ܦܩܕ ܐܢܐ ܕܬܦܠ.

86. ܦܘܩܐ ܕܝܢ ܡܙܝܥܐ ܒܒܪ ܫܠܡܬܐ ܕܡܪܗ. ܘܥܠ
ܠܒܢܐ ܘܡܕܡܪܐ ܗܘܬ ܗ، ܒܢܐ ܐܝܟ ܚܣܝܐ ܡܢ
ܢܘܪܐ. ܘܟܕ ܡܢ ܒܡܨܥܬܐ ܥܒܪ، ܕܒܪܢܝ ܘܐܡܪ
ܡܘܕܐ | ܐܢܐ ܠܟ ܡܪܢܐ ܕܐܫܬܘܬܦܬܢ ܠܐܣܘܪܐ B 231r.1
ܘܠܦܓܪܐ ܕܒܝܬ ܐܣܝܪܐ ܘܠܣܘܪܩܐ ܘܠܚܫ̈ܘܟܐ
ܫܢ̈ܩܐ ܘܡܚܘܬܐ ܡܪܢܐ ܥܒܕ ܡܠܐܟܐ[258]
ܘܦܨܝܗ ܡܢ ܐܝ̈ܕܘܗܝ، ܕܛܪܝܢܘܣ ܕܠܐ ܢܡܪܘܩ
ܒܡ̈ܠܟܐ ܕܐܝܟܘ ܐܠܗܗ.

87. ܒܪ ܕܝܢ ܥܠܡ ܒܠܬܗ ܘܐܣܩ ܬܫܒܘܚܬܐ
ܕܫܘܠܡܗ ܒܪ ܐܡܝܢ ܐܫܠܡ ܢܦܫܗ ܒܡܕܢܚ
ܫܡܫܐ. ܘܦܩܕ | ܛܪܝܢܘܣ ܕܬܬܦܬܚ ܒܢܐ A 211r.1
ܘܐܫܬܟܚ ܦܓܪܗ ܕܛܘܒܢܐ ܦܘܩܐ ܐܝܟ ܢܪܕܝܢ
ܥܦܝܪܐ ܘܡܪܓܠܝܛܐ. ܘܐܝܟ ܒܣܡܐ ܢܦܝܩ
ܕܒ̈ܝܫܐ. ܘܐܫܬܟܚܬ ܒܢܐ ܐܝܟ ܗܘ ܕܡܟܬܫ
ܠܐ ܐܫܬܓܪܬ.

88. ܘܟܕ ܚܙܐ ܛܪܝܢܘܣ ܥܒܕܗ ܕܛܘܒܢܐ ܦܘܩܐ ܡܟܐ
ܘܐܡܪ ܠܘܬ ܐܣܛܪܛܝܘܛܘܗܝ، ܚܙܘ
ܒܫܒܪܘܬܗ ܕܗܢܐ ܘܕܗܝܡܢܘܬܗ[259]. ܥܪܝܪܐܝܬ

256 ܕܬܫܬܡܠܐ
257 = B; A ܥܒܪ ܐܢܐ
258 ܡܠܐܟܝܢ
259 ܗܝܡܢܘܬܗ

TEXT 53

ܠܝܬ ܐܠܗ ܐܚܪܝܢ ܐܠܐ ܐܒܗܬܐ ܕܗܢܘܢ.²⁶⁰
ܘܒܪܘܬܐ ܒܪܝܗ ܗܘܐ.

89. ܘܗܘܐ ܡܢ ܒܬܪ ܕܥܠ ܠܘܬܗ܂ ܘܡܕܡ²⁶¹,
ܗܘܐ²⁶² ܩܒܠܗ ܠܗ ܘܐܡܪ ܐܢܬܝ | ܠܝ
ܠܐܝܬܐ ܕܝܕܥܬ ܠܝ܂ ܠܡܢܐܕܘ ܐܬܒܬ
ܐܢܬܝ ܒܛܠܠ ܠܐ ܓܝܪ ܐܝܬܝ ܠܡܘܬ
ܕܚܝܘܬܐ ܒܪܗ ܗܐ ܥܠܝܟܝ²⁶³. ܘܫܒܩܬ
ܐܢܬܝ ܠܐܠܗܐ ܚܝܐ ܗܘܡܬ ܒܚܝ ܠܓܒܪܐ²⁶⁴
ܐܠܐ ܐܠܗܐ ܬܒܥ ܗܕܐ ܓܝܪ ܐܬܝܬ
ܕܐܦܪܘܥܝܟܝ.

90. ܘܟܕ²⁶⁵ ܫܡܥܬ ܗܕܐ ܒܪ ܠܝܠܝܬ ܐܚܕܗ
ܐܪܘܝܬܐ܂ ܘܗܘܘ ܚܙܝܗ ܕܪܗܒܘܢ ܡܢ |
ܗܕܡܝܗ ܚܝܘܗܝ ܥܩܡ.

91. ܗܘ ܐܓܠܝܐ ܡܠܟ ܐܝܟ ܣܓܝ ܘܡܐ ܙܡܪܐ,
ܗܘܐ܂ ܘܡܪܝܕܘ ܐܡܪ ܩܒܠܝܗ܂ ܘܫܬܠܐܢ
ܕܐܡܪܐ ܠܢܒܝܐ ܕܪܗܒܘܢ ܠܡܠܟܐ ܗܠܟ
ܘܡܪܝܒܘܐ ܕܐܠܗܐ܂ ܘܐܡܪ ܕܢܝܕ܂ ܡܛܠܟ ܣܒܝܗ
ܘܬܪܗܡ ܠܟܠܗ ܕܒܝܬܗ ܐܠܗ ܘܡܘܗܒܬܐ܂
ܕܐܢܫܝܢ, ܡܥܒܕ ܪܚܡܬܐ ܕܐܝܠܝܢ
ܘܛܦܝܗ ܕܒܣܘܛܐ ܥܠܝܟ ܠܗ ܬܥܠ
ܕܢܘܚܝ²⁶⁶ ܐܚܝܕܟܝ ܕܐܝܟ ܕܥܠܝܟ | ܘܡܘܒܠ
ܟܠܗ ܕܐܗܘܬܐ ܡܢ ܓܘܝܗ ܗܘ ܗܝ ܣܘܒܐ
ܘܒܝܠܟܐ ܒܕ ܙܡܪܐ ܘܚܝ ܕܢܘܚܝ ܥܠ ܟܠܗ
ܐܡܪ²⁶⁷

ܫܠܡ²⁶⁸

---

²⁶⁰ = B; A ܐܠܗܐ
²⁶¹ = B; A + ܠܗ
²⁶² + ܒܢܝܐ
²⁶³ + sey.
²⁶⁴ ܠܓܒܪܘܬܝ
²⁶⁵ ܗܘ ܕܝܢܘܗܝ
²⁶⁶ om. sey.
²⁶⁷ + ܘܐܡܪ
²⁶⁸ ܫܠܡ ܡܘܠܕܗ ܕܝܘܚܢܢ ܡܥܡܕܢܐ

BIBLIOGRAPHY

ANCIENT TEXTS

Acta Sanctorum, Mensis Iulius III (Antwerp, 1723).
Asterius, *Homily* 4: ed. C. Datema, C. Datema, *Asterius of Amasea, Homilies I–XIV* (Leiden, 1970).
Gregory of Nazianzus, *Poems*, Patrologia Graeca 37.
John Chrysostom, *Homily on St Phokas*, Patrologia Graeca 50, 699–706
Martyrologes et ménologes orientaux. Un martyrologe et douze ménologes syriaques, ed. F. Nau, Patrologia Orientalis 10:1 (1912).
Severus, *Homily* 72: ed. M. Brière, Patrologia Orientalis 12:1 (1907).
Synaxarium Ecclesiae Constantinopolitanae, ed. H. Delehaye (Bruxelles, 1902).
Vark' ew vkayabanutiwnk' srboc', II (Venice, 1874).

MODERN LITERATURE

F. C. Conybeare, *The Armenian Apology and Acts of Apollonius and other Monuments of Early Christianity* (2nd edn. London, 1896).
B. Dehandschutter, (translation of Asterius, Homily IV), in J. Leemans and other, *Homilies on Christian Martyrs* (London, 2003), pp. 167–73.
W. Enslin, Paulys *Real-enzyklopädie der classischen Altertumswissenschaft* 20 (1940), cols. 451–2 ('Phokas 11').
J-M. Fiey, 'De quelques saints vénérés au Liban', *Proche Orient Chrétien* 28 (1978), pp. 18–43.
— (ed. L.I. Conrad), *Saints syriaques* (Princeton, 2004). [Arabic edition, Beirut, 2005].
G. Garitte, *Le calendrier palestino-géorgien du Sinaiticus 34 (Xe siècle)* (Subsidia Hagiographica 30; Bruxelles, 1958).
J. Leemans, W. Mayer, P. Allen and B. Dehandschutter, *'Let us die that we may live'. Greek Homilies on Christian Martyrs from Asia Minor, Palestine and Syriac (c. AD 35–AD 450)* (London, 2003).

N. Oikonomides, Ὁ Ἅγιος Φωκᾶς ὁ Σινωπεύς, *Archeion Pontou* 17 (1952), pp. 184–219.

P. Peeters, 'Le martyrologie de Rabban Sliba', *Analecta Bollandiana* 27 (1908), pp. 129–200.

H. Pognon, *Inscriptions sémitiques de la Syrie, de la Mésopotamie, et de la région de Mossoul* (Paris, 1907).

J-M. Sauget, 'Focas', in *Bibliotheca Sanctorum* 5 (Rome, 1964), cols 948–50.

—'Le calendrier maronite du manuscrit Vatican syriaque 313', *Orientalia Christiana Periodica* 33 (1967), pp. 221–93.

M. Tarchnishvili, *Geschichte der kirchlichen georgischen Literatur* (Studi e Testi 185; 1955).

C. van de Vorst, 'Saint Phocas', *Analecta Bollandiana* 30 (1911), pp. 252–95.

INDEX OF NAMES

Africanus	4–47 passim
Aristotle	24, 25
Armenia	1, 91
Asklepiades	57
Cappadocia	1
Crispinus	71
Demosthenes	38, 41
Galatia	1
Jews	27
Mysia	1
Paphlagonia	1, 91
Phokas	passim
Pontus	1, 91
Poseidon	61, 75
Terentina	47
Trajan	9, 49–90 passim

Index of Biblical References

Ex. 14:16	80
I Sam. 2:6	35
2 Kgs 5:7	35
Job 5:13	17
Ps. 79(78):10	86
Ps. 80(79):15	72
Ps. 93(92):4	46
Ps. 97(96):5	80
Is. 29:14	17
Is. 50:2	80
Dan. 2:21	17
I Macc. 3:18 etc	7
II Macc. 3:30 etc.	7
Mt. 7:6	64
Mt. 11:29	3
Mt. 13:45	43
Mt. 13:46	73
Mt. 27:19	47
Acts 12:23	90
Acts 16:25–33	74
I Cor. 1:19	7
I Cor. 1:23	27
I Cor. 3:19	7
I Cor. 10:33	3
Eph. 1:21	72
Rev. 5:9	72

Index of Greek Words

68	(ἀήρ)	ܐܐܪ
1, 3, 75, 91	(ἀγών)	ܐܓܘܢܐ
11	(σχῆμα)	ܐܣܟܡܐ
33	(στοιχεῖον)	ܐܣܛܘܟܣܐ
35	(στρατία)	ܐܣܛܪܛܝܐ
71, 74, 88	(στρατιώτης)	ܐܣܛܪܛܝܘܛܐ
13	(ἐπίσκοπος)	ܐܦܣܩܘܦܐ
1	(ἀθλητής)	ܐܬܠܝܛܐ
85–87	(βαλανεῖον)	ܒܠܢܐ
1, 4	(γένος)	ܓܢܣܐ
2	(ὑπομνήματα)	ܗܘܦܡܢܡܛܐ
5, 13	(ἔπαρχος)	ܗܘܦܪܟܐ
1	(τύπος)	ܛܘܦܣܐ
89	(τύραννος)	ܛܪܘܢܐ
20	(τέχνη)	ܛܟܢܐ
59	(ναός)	ܢܘܣܐ
18, 19, 27, 74	(νόμος)	ܢܡܘܣܐ
73	(ἄσημον)	ܣܐܡܐ
14, 15	(συνήγορος)	ܣܢܐܓܪܐ
1, 2	(πολιτεία)	ܦܘܠܝܛܝܐ
25	(φιλόσοφος)	ܦܝܠܣܘܦܐ
24, 55, 79	(φιλόσοφος)	ܦܝܠܘܣܘܦܐ
19, 20, 73	(πεῖσαι)	ܐܦܝܣ (:ܦܝܣ)
18, 38		ܐܬܛܦܝܣ

90	(παλάτιον)	ܦܠܛܝܢ
78	(πρόνοος)	ܦܪܢܘ
62	(κυβερνήτης)	ܩܘܒܪܢܝܛܐ
74	(κανδήλας)	ܩܢܕܝܠܐ
71	(κεντυρίων)	ܩܢܛܪܘܢܐ
87	(κρύσταλλος)	ܩܪܘܣܛܠܐ
91	(τάγμα)	ܛܓܡܐ